Chaldeans in Michigan

Discovering the Peoples of Michigan is a series of publications examining the state's rich multicultural heritage. The series makes available an interesting, affordable, and varied collection of books that enables students and lay readers to explore Michigan's ethnic dynamics. A knowledge of the state's rapidly changing multicultural history has far-reaching implications for human relations, education, public policy, and planning. We believe that Discovering the Peoples of Michigan will enhance understanding of the unique contributions that diverse and often unrecognized communities have made to Michigan's history and culture.

Chaldeans in Michigan

Mary C. Sengstock

Michigan State University Press

East Lansing

⊗ The paper used in this publication meets the minimum requirements
of ANSI/NISO Z39.48-1992 (R 1997) (Permanence of Paper)

Michigan State University Press
East Lansing, Michigan 48823-5245

Printed and bound in the United States of America
12 11 10 09 08 07 06 05   1 2 3 4 5 6 7 8 9 10

LIBRARY OF CONGRESS CATALOGING-IN-PUBLICATION DATA
Sengstock, Mary C.
Chaldeans in Michigan / Mary C. Sengstock.
p. cm.—(Discovering the peoples of Michigan)
Includes bibliographical references and index.
ISBN 0-87013-742-5 (alk. paper)
1. Chaldean Catholics—Michigan—History. 2. Chaldean Catholics—Michigan—
Social conditions. 3. Chaldean Catholics—Michigan—Detroit—History. 4. Immigrants—
Michigan—History. 5. Michigan—Ethnic relations. 6. Michigan—Social conditions.
7. Detroit (Mich.)—Ethnic relations. I. Title. II. Series.
F575.C36S46 2005
977.4'004927567—dc22
2004029211

Discovering the Peoples of Michigan. The editors wish
to thank the Kellogg Foundation for their generous support.

Cover design by Ariana Grabec-Dingman
Book design by Sharp Des!gns, Lansing, Michigan

Visit Michigan State University Press on the World Wide Web at
www.msupress.msu.edu

SERIES ACKNOWLEDGMENTS

Discovering the Peoples of Michigan is a series of publications that resulted from the cooperation and effort of many individuals. The people recognized here are not a complete representation, for the list of contributors is too numerous to mention. However, credit must be given to Jeffrey Bonevich, who worked tirelessly with me on contacting people as well as researching and organizing material.

The initial idea for this project came from Mary Erwin, but I must thank Fred Bohm, director of the Michigan State University Press, for seeing the need for this project, for giving it his strong support, and for making publication possible. Also, the tireless efforts of Keith Widder and Elizabeth Demers, senior editors at Michigan State University Press, were vital in bringing DPOM to fruition.

Otto Feinstein and Germaine Strobel of the Michigan Ethnic Heritage Studies Center patiently and willingly provided names for contributors and constantly gave this project their tireless support. Yvonne Lockwood of the Michigan State University Museum has also suggested and advised contributors.

Many of the maps in the series were prepared by Gregory Anderson at the Geographical Information Center (GIS) at Western Michigan University under the directorship of David Dickason. Additional maps have been contributed by Ellen White.

Other authors and organizations provided comments on other aspects of the work. There are many people that were interviewed by the various authors who will remain anonymous. However, they have enabled the story of their group to be told. Unfortunately, their names are not available, but we are grateful for their cooperation.

Most of all, this work is a tribute to the writers who patiently gave their time to write and share their research findings. Their contributions are noted and appreciated. To them goes most of the gratitude.

ARTHUR W. HELWEG, *Series Co-editor*

Contents

Introduction

The term "Chaldean," to most Americans, conjures up long-forgotten images from ancient history lessons or Sunday School Bible stories. Abraham's home was in Ur of the Chaldees, although this is somewhat anachronistic, since Ur was part of Babylon at that time, and Chaldean control over the area did not occur until about a thousand years later. North of Ur lies the valley of the Tigris and Euphrates Rivers, often identified as the "cradle of civilization." This area, known as the "Fertile Crescent" and located in what is now the nation of Iraq, was the heart of the ancient civilization of Mesopotamia and the Assyrian and Babylonian empires.

What have the ancient Chaldeans and Assyrians to do with Metropolitan Detroit at the dawn of a new millennium? After all, they existed so long ago—five or six millennia in the past. What have they to do with modern America? Their relevance lies in the fact that a community of persons who claim to be the modern day descendants of these ancient people has been a part of the Detroit Metropolitan area since the early part of the twentieth century. After five thousand years, the legitimacy of their claim is almost impossible to document. As Karoukian indicates, scholars who focus on Assyrian history are often not receptive to the claims of present-day descendants from these ancient peoples.[1]

Iraq, Showing Chaldeans' Home Village of Telkaif. Mary C. Sengstock, Chaldean-Americans: Changing Conceptions of Ethnic Identity, *2d ed. (New York: Center for Migration Studies, 1999). Reprinted with permission of the publisher.*

What is certain, however, is that the Detroit Chaldean community originates from a town called Telkaif (pronounced T'l *kef* or *T'l* kef), located in the Tigris River region near Mosul and the ruins of the ancient Assyrian city of Nineveh. The town is called "Telkeppa," meaning "rocky" in the Chaldean language, a reference to the rocky hill on which the town is situated.[2] Even today, most of Detroit's Chaldeans can trace their ancestry to the town of Telkaif. Perhaps 5 percent are descended from residents of other Iraqi towns, most also located in the same province of Mosul.

Chaldeans are proud of their descent from the ancient peoples of Chaldea and Babylonia. In ancient Babylonia, the arrival of a new year was a time of great celebration with the arrival of spring. This depiction of the ancient Babylonian new year celebration appeared in the Chaldean community calendar for April 2002. ("Calendar of the Chaldean People of Ancient Babylonia," published by the Chaldean Educational Center in Metropolitan Detroit, 2002. Reprinted with permission.)

Based upon this geographic origin, Chaldeans also lay claim to the "Assyrian" and "Babylonian" titles from the pre-Christian era. The Assyrian king, Ashurbanipal, ruled the area of the Tigris-Euphrates Valley from the ancient city of Nineveh in the seventh century B.C. (668–627).[3] The ruins of Nineveh are located less than fifty miles from the Detroit Chaldeans' home village of Telkaif.[4]

Early Beginnings of Detroit's Chaldean Community

The first Chaldean known to have come to the United States was Zia Attalla, who arrived in Philadelphia in 1889. He worked in a hotel there and later returned to the Middle East and opened a hotel in Baghdad.[5] The first Chaldeans to come to Detroit came in the early 1900s. There are community reports of a Chaldean immigrant to Detroit in 1908, and perhaps of another as early 1905. Efforts to document the accuracy of these claims and the identity of the immigrants are currently under way in the community.

From a population of only twenty-three in 1923, the Chaldean community in Michigan has grown considerably over the past century. Current population figures are highly debated. Church records indicate a population of over 100,000, nearly all concentrated in the Detroit Metropolitan area.[6] Many outsiders insist that the number is far lower; but most are unaware of the many subgroups and areas in which Chaldeans reside. The earliest Chaldean immigrants were primarily male, as was common among immigrants in the late nineteenth and early twentieth centuries. It is uncertain why the first Chaldeans chose to come to Detroit as opposed to other parts of the United States. However, the early decades of the twentieth century were the period in which the automobile industry was growing in Detroit, creating a magnet for immigrants. Detroit also already had the nucleus of a community of Middle Eastern immigrants, with a number of immigrants from Greater Syria, including modern Syria and Lebanon. It is possible that word of this developing Middle Eastern population had reached other parts of the Middle East by this time.

If the reason for the first Chaldean's choice of Detroit is uncertain, the reason for all subsequent ones is not. Once there were a few Chaldeans in Detroit, others were likely to follow. In the earliest years, Chaldeans often associated with those of Lebanese or Syrian ancestry. This was not surprising in view of the fact that both groups came from Arabic-speaking areas of the Middle East, and both practiced variations of the Roman Catholic religion. Within a few decades, however, the Chaldean community grew to a sufficient size that its members operated as an independent community.

A Profile of Detroit's Chaldeans

Chaldeans are considered to be immigrants from Iraq, although Iraq as a nation did not exist at the time the early immigrants left their native village.[7] In many respects, the Chaldeans represent a minority within the Iraqi population. Most notable is their religious affiliation. Unlike

ܢܚܦ ܕܢܒܝܠܗ ܚܥܦܢܐ. ܦܝܟ ܡܣܡܘܕܟܐ ܚܡܘܗܓ. ܢܡܢܗ ܡܠܟܘܡܗܘܗ.
ܗܘܐ ܠܝܚܦܢܘܗ. ܕܢܒܝ ܕܢܒܝܠܗ ܕܢܒܝ ܚܥܦܢܐ ܗܘܕܢܒܝ ܗܡ ܕܢܕܐܟܐ. ܘܓܟܠ
ܠܣܚܐ ܗܘܢܦܢܒ ܠܕܢܡܘܡܙ. ܡܥܚܦܡ ܝܟܠ ܠܢܗܝ ܡܢܗܝܢܝܟ. ܕܢܒܝ
ܕܘܗܡ ܢܚܒ ܥܚܢܡܠ ܗܙ ܢܒܬ ܕܡܗܘܡܒܘܒܠܬ ܝܟܠ. ܘܟܐ ܡܬܒܝܕܗ.
ܚܝܘܕܢܐ. ܝܟܐ ܡܚܟܝ ܟܡ ܡܓ ܚܒܐ. ܡܗܒܬ ܕܝܘܗܓ ܢܒܟܗ ܡܠܟܚܘܡܗܙ
ܘܢܢܠܐ ܘܗܥܚܦܢܡܣܐ ܠܢܕܘ ܢܚܕܒ ܢܗܣ.

أبانا ألذي في السماوات ليتقدس إسمك ليأتي ملكوتك لتكن مشيئتك كما
في السماء كذلك على الأرض. أعطنا خبزنا كفافنا أليوم وأغفر لنا
ذنوبنا وخطايانا كما نحن أيضاً نغفر لمن أخطأ إلينا. ولا تدخلنا في
التجربة لكن نجنا من الشرير لأن لك ألملك والقوة والتسبحة إلى آبد
ألآبدين آمين.

Two quite different languages have been spoken by members of the Chaldean community. The earliest immigrants, who came from the village of Telkaif, spoke Chaldean, a modern-day version of Aramaic, the language spoken by Christ. Recent immigrants, who were reared in modern-day Iraq and educated in Iraqi schools, are more likely to speak Arabic, the national language of Iraq. In recent years, Chaldean leaders have introduced classes to revive the Chaldean language among both immigrants and American-born Chaldeans.

Both languages are written from right to left, rather than left to right, as in English. However, the script used in writing the two languages is quite different, as can be seen from these examples. The two passages given here are both the Lord's Prayer ("Our Father"). The passage at the top is in Chaldean (Aramaic); the passage below is in Arabic.

the majority of the population of Iraq and its surrounding countries, Chaldeans are not Muslims but are Christians, practicing a special ritual pattern (or "rite") of the Roman Catholic Church.[8]

In their ancestral language they diverge as well. For Chaldeans in Iraq, Arabic was not their first language. Telkeffes or Telkeppes, as residents of Telkaif are called, speak a language that is a modern variant of ancient Aramaic, also called Syriac, Assyrian, after the Assyrian Empire that once dominated the area, or "Jesus' language," in deference to the fact that Aramaic was the language allegedly spoken by Jesus during his life. Most Chaldean immigrants today have been educated in Iraqi schools and speak Arabic, the dominant language of Iraq. Indeed, many do not even know the Chaldean language. However, there is still a strong commitment to the Chaldean language, much like the Irish commitment to the Gaelic language, though English is now the predominant language in Ireland, and though many Irish do not speak Gaelic.

Chaldean Migration to the United States

Once Chaldeans began coming to Detroit, their numbers increased quickly. By 1943 the community numbered more than nine hundred.[9] Twenty years later there were over three hundred families, with approximately three thousand persons, in the community.[10] The size of the current population has been a matter of dispute since the change in immigration laws in 1965.[11] Estimates differ dramatically, and an accurate count that satisfies everyone is probably impossible to achieve. In 1986, for example, a Detroit area community-planning organization estimated the entire Arabic speaking population of the Metropolitan Detroit Area at seventy-eight thousand, and the Chaldean population at about ten thousand.[12] An earlier analysis, however, estimated Detroit's Arabic population at about two hundred thousand,[13] suggesting that the enumeration of the entire Arabic population in the Detroit area was probably vastly underestimated.

Studies providing the lower population figures, such as the one cited here, came primarily from U.S. Census data. Census Bureau statistics are problematic for workers and researchers familiar with Detroit's Arabic population, for a variety of reasons. The data are notably unreliable for most minority groups, a fact that has led to considerable pressure on the U.S. Census Bureau to modify its techniques to assure a more complete count of minority groups and the poor, who may have unstable residential patterns and a distrust of government agencies.[14]

Newcomers in particular often live with a variety of relatives, who may not be certain whether the individual should be counted. They (like many immigrants) also bring with them from their homeland a

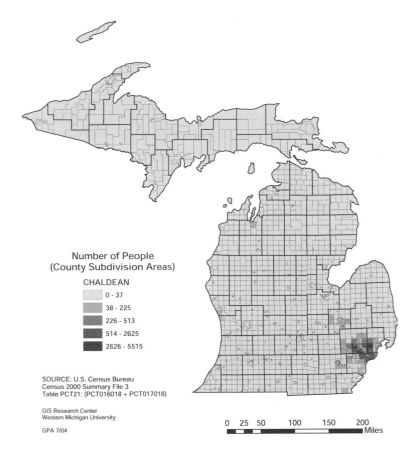

Number of People
(County Subdivision Areas)
CHALDEAN

- 0 - 37
- 38 - 225
- 226 - 513
- 514 - 2625
- 2626 - 5515

SOURCE: U.S. Census Bureau
Census 2000 Summary File 3
Table PCT21: (PCT016018 + PCT017018)

GIS Research Center
Western Michigan University

GPA 7/04

0   25   50   100   150   200
Miles

Distribution of Michigan's Population Claiming Chaldean Ancestry.

substantial mistrust of governmental power, resulting in an unwilling-
ness to respond to questions from government agencies. This is particularly true if some members of the family may be in the United States
illegally. Finally, there is resistance on the part of many Chaldeans to
the way they are asked to identify themselves. For several decades the
term "Chaldean" was rejected as a category of ethnic identity by the
Census Bureau, on the grounds that it was primarily a religious designation rather than a nationality. Consequently, Chaldeans had to select

another category by which to identify themselves. Options were
Assyrian, Arab, or Iraqi, all of which were resisted by many of them—
and embraced by others. The cumulative result of these factors has
been what community leaders claim is a considerable undercount of
the Chaldean population in the U.S. Census.

This situation was changed with the 2000 Census, when the Census
was persuaded by community leaders to accept their view that they are
in fact an ethnic group. Of major importance in the Census Bureau's
policy change were historical and sociological analyses of the Chaldean
community. These statements pointed out the extensive pre-Christian
origins of the Chaldean peoples, as well as the broad-based status of
the current community, including the breadth of institutions it exhibits,
the genealogical connection of the members, and the similarity to other
ethnic groups, in which religion is but a single factor in community
identity. It was also pointed out that conversion is a common method
of population growth in religious communities, but one cannot "con-
vert" to an ethnic group.[15]

Persons familiar with the Arabic-speaking communities tend to
use their own estimates of the population. The Chaldean Church listed
about 65,000 persons as members in 1998.[16] Father Manuel Boji of the
main Chaldean diocesan parish estimated the population in early 2003
at approximately 120,000, based on the requests received for church
services such as baptisms and funerals.[17] The Chaldean community in
Detroit is the single major concentration of Chaldeans outside of the
Middle East. Other concentrations exist in Spring Valley, California, a
suburb of San Diego, in Phoenix, Arizona, and in Mexico, and have
close ties to the Detroit community, since their residents are also primarily of Telkeffe ancestry. Concentrations of Christians with similar
cultural backgrounds who originate from other parts of the Middle East
reside in Chicago, Illinois, and Turlock, California, but most of them are
more likely to identify themselves as Assyrians than Chaldeans.

Chaldeans in the Detroit area are concentrated in the north-cen-
tral portion of the city (near John R and Seven Mile Roads), as well as in
several suburbs in Oakland County to the north of Detroit, notably Oak
Park, Southfield, Farmington, Farmington Hills, Birmingham, Bloomfield, Bloomfield Hills, West Bloomfield, and Troy (see map). The John

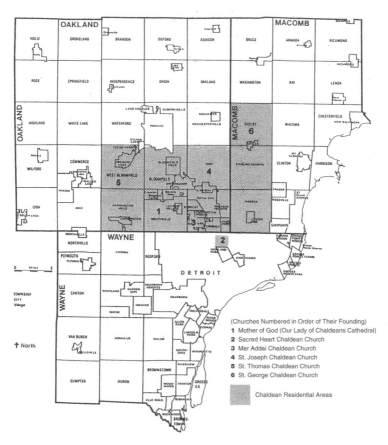

Major Residential Areas of Chaldeans in Detroit Metropolitan Area, Including Location of Six Chaldean Churches. Mary C. Sengstock, Chaldean-Americans: Changing Conceptions of Ethnic Identity, *2d ed. (New York: Center for Migration Studies, 1999). Reprinted with permission of the publisher.*

R-Seven Mile Road segment of the community consists primarily of recent immigrants. As these new arrivals become more established and prosperous, many join their predecessors in the suburbs. Some immigrants who have been preceded by numerous relations may bypass the central city area of first settlement and immediately move in with their suburban relatives. This is a common pattern in the community today.

Chaldean migration to the Detroit area provides an excellent example of what has been called "chain migration."[18] Migration, like other social phenomena, does not occur in a vacuum, but rather within the social context of the group. Hence the migration of a single individual begins a long-term pattern in which additional persons from the original town or community follow the first to the same area.

The urge for migrants to bring families and friends to join them is strong. Migration can be a lonesome process, since it constitutes what has been called a "shrinking social field."[19] Old roles and relationships are gone. People who are used to having parents, siblings, and cousins to depend upon to assist with problems, or even the activities of daily life, must find new social contacts and solutions. Men may have been involved in economic ventures with fathers, brothers, or cousins. Women often depended upon mothers, sisters, and cousins to assist with childcare and household chores. After immigration, all of these patterns must be replaced, and ethnic communities often fill this void. Among Chaldeans, it was not really necessary to develop a sense of community in the United States—they simply brought their old community with them, in the person of their relatives and neighbors.

In the early years of Chaldean migration to Detroit, the first person from a family to arrive was usually a male, traveling alone. The Thomas Hakim family is a good example. Hakim came to the United States in 1923, traveling through Mexico to Detroit. Having established himself in the grocery business, he returned to Telkaif to bring his wife, Barbara, and their two sons. Several years later he took his oldest son, Karim, back to Telkaif to obtain a wife. Karim married Naima (Norma) Dalaly, the daughter of Thomas Hakim's former business partner in Telkaif. Once Norma had become a citizen, she was able to assist her own brothers in coming to the United States, along with their own wives and children. The chain could continue indefinitely, and this pattern has been followed by most immigrant communities in the United States. In the Chaldean community, the chain often included Chaldeans from parts of the world other than the Middle East. For example, one member of the Hakim family married a woman from the Chaldean community in Oaxaca, Mexico.

The advantages of chain migration are many. Perhaps the most obvious is the fact that American immigration laws, for many years, gave preference in obtaining immigrant visas to persons who already had relatives in the United States. Another advantage is the economic assistance that can be provided by relatives and friends already in the United States, such as helping the immigrant to find a job once he or she arrives in this country, a topic that will be discussed later. A more subtle, but very important type of advantage provided by chain migration is simply informational—it is easier to move to a new country if one already has relatives there to help pave the way.

Culture and Institutions in the Chaldean Community

Over time, Chaldeans developed a strong set of institutions to unite the community. The major institutions of the community are the church, the family, and the retail grocery business. The earliest immigrants brought religious and family institutions with them when they came from their homeland. However, one of the first tasks they faced in the new country was the need to find a way to make a living, and a common economic institution resulted from this need. The following pages will focus on these three institutions, an analysis of which is critical to understanding the Chaldean community.

The Chaldean Family

If there is a central focus to the Chaldean community, it is the family. One cannot discuss Chaldean life without referring to the family. In Telkaif, men attained status by virtue of the number of children they had, as well as the number of other relatives they were supporting. In 1962, the median family size in the Detroit community was 5.6.[20] Many families had eight or more children. Families are large, even today. The original village of Telkaif was endogamous, and residents often referred to each other as *nashwatha* ("cousins"), since everyone was seen to be related to everyone else in the town.

The extended family of grandparents, aunts, uncles, cousins, and other relatives plays an extremely important role in the lives of Chaldeans. Marriages within the Chaldean community are preferred, and many Chaldeans, even those born and reared in America, follow their parents' wishes and marry within the community. Although those who do not are not ostracized. Instead, the non-Chaldean spouse will usually be encouraged to become a full-fledged participant in the Chaldean extended family. Chaldean families are characterized by strong bonds among the members, a great deal of interchange of assistance—what anthropologists tend to call the "functionally extended family"—and even the sharing of a single household by members of the extended family. In other respects as well, Chaldean families exercise considerable influence over their members. Many young people, for example, have been known to forgo their own career choices in order to follow their parents' preference that they remain in the family business, a topic that will be discussed later. Chaldean families also tend to exhibit traditional role differentiation along gender lines.

Original Chaldean Families

The family structure that early Chaldean immigrants brought with them from Iraq had a three part focus. It was patrilineal, with the emphasis on the father's line. Inheritance passed through the father, not the mother, and when a girl married, she joined her husband's family, although she was always considered to be descended from her father. The family was also extended: it included a broad range of relatives, including grandparents, siblings, aunts, uncles, and cousins. Often these relatives were included in the household, but at the least, there was frequent visiting, and deeply felt obligations to them. These obligations were so strong that many elderly Chaldean men in the old country were caring for a wide variety of other relatives, including aged parents, unmarried sisters, and widowed sisters-in-law and their children. Men who accepted these obligations were highly respected in the community, and they referred to their dependents as *ardagh*, or "my dignity."

Finally, there was also a strong sentiment in favor of endogamy; that is, children were expected to marry within the family network, with marriage between cousins being common. Of course, all of these dimensions complemented each other. If children married cousins, the daughter might not be "lost" to another family, the father's family's wealth would not be depleted, and people could feel comfortable living with or assisting other members of the family. Chaldean families are also relatively large. Some immigrants report having had as many as a dozen brothers and sisters. However, a change in family size in modern America was obvious in the study of elderly Chaldeans in 1990–91, who reported an average of 5.2 children. A few had as many as 14 or 15. Their children, however, are approaching the American ideal of two or three children.

It is questionable how accurate this picture of the family in the old country is, but it is the ideal pattern that the immigrants brought with them, and that they attempted to reproduce in the United States. Early immigrants tried to impress upon their children their responsibility to remain close to the extended family, even to the extent of pressuring young married couples to live with the husband's parents after marriage and to become involved in the family business and other family activities.

This pattern has changed a great deal over the past century, in Iraq as well as in the United States. For example, most couples today do not actually live with their parents after marriage. Few young couples favor the idea of joining their parents in a common household, although some experience parental pressure to do so. It is also clear, however, that many older Chaldeans, having been born in the United States, or at least having lived here for many years, are no more interested than their children in living in joint households. While many Chaldeans, like other groups before them, see these changes as "Americanization," they are more likely to be a characteristic pattern of the industrialized, urbanized environment, which is occurring all over the world.

Continued Extended Family Contact and Influence

Despite trends of Americanization, Chaldeans in Detroit appear more likely to live with extended family members than are other Americans.

In the original village of Telkaif, when a woman married, she was arrayed in bright colors and golden jewelry. Here Mary Yasso is pictured dressed for her wedding to Mansour Bashi in Telkaif in 1960. (Photo compliments of Rev. Jacob Yasso. Published with permission of Michigan History.)

The contrast between village and urban life is visible in this picture of Mary and Mansour Bashi with their daughter, Bushra, four years after their marriage, after moving to Baghdad. (Photo compliments of Rev. Jacob Yasso. Published with permission of Michigan History.)

A particularly interesting pattern might be called a "sometimes extended family household." That is, Chaldean couples are likely to include within the household other relatives in need of a place to live. This is particularly true for elderly parents, but may also include new immigrants, cousins attending school, visitors from the old country or other parts of the United States, and so on. Placing an elderly parent in a nursing home is quite rare among Chaldeans, and is considered most inappropriate. This has changed somewhat, however, with the establishment of senior citizens' housing in close proximity to the main Chaldean Church.

Family visits may extend from a few months to several years. In one case, a social worker in a medical facility became concerned because family members claimed that an elderly relative had "come down with Alzheimer's disease" while visiting a son in another state. The social worker questioned the accuracy of the account, because Alzheimer's disease is a chronic, degenerative disease with a long-term onset. How could one "come down with it" over the course of a visit? However, this is understandable in the context of this community, in which a "visit" may extend over a two- to three-year period!

Having other relatives living with them is particularly common among couples in which one partner is foreign born. Many of these couples initially started out as "passport marriages," in which one partner, usually the husband, was admitted to the United States as the spouse of an American citizen. The foreign-born partner nearly always has relatives remaining in Iraq, and is usually anxious to have them join him (or, less frequently, her) in the United States. Clearly it is more economical for them to have these relatives live with them in their early years in this country. Usually these arrangements are temporary, but in some instances these "temporary" arrangements may last for several years, until the newcomers become well enough established to form their own homes.

Even when they do not share the same household, it is clear that Chaldean families in the United States remain exceptionally close to their extended families. This extended family pattern manifests itself in many ways. For example, Chaldean couples feel a strong responsibility to provide care for their parents in old age, even when they do not share a household. When the families have separate households, they are likely to locate their homes close to other family members. In many instances, families will deliberately select homes in newly developing subdivisions, in order to assure that several members of the extended family can purchase adjoining lots on which to build. Detroit's Chaldean families are also what Farsoun called a "functionally extended family," in which members may not live together, but they engage in a wide range of joint activities: cooking and caring for each others' children, operating businesses together, and so on.[21] In an interview with *Crain's Detroit Business,* Chaldean attorney Salman Sesi indicated that Chaldean families often help each other to come to the United States, as well as to obtain the necessary skills to establish a business.[22] The number of persons included in these activities is large, and extends not only to persons in the Detroit area, but also to those in other parts of the United States and the world.[23]

As in most extended family systems, members of the extended family expect to be included in the lives of their members. Young Chaldeans are heavily pressured to consider family preferences in their choice of a job or a spouse—and many of them report that they expect to do so. When interviewing Chaldeans, researchers frequently find that other members of the family or community will come over to the house to see who is visiting and why, and will often join in the interview—an unusual alternative to common social scientific research techniques that assume an *individual* interview! This illustrates, however, the intimate character of Chaldean family structure, in which it is assumed that members operate as part of the group, and that there are no secrets from the extended family.

Ethnic families are often of great assistance to their members. Economic assistance is a primary example. Chaldean families are a major source of loans for their members, and many Chaldeans are in joint business activities with relatives. For example, Lane chronicles the family of James Jonna, president of Jonna Companies, who came to the United States and got his start in the grocery business. He then moved on to establish a major development and construction company, which included his son, two daughters, and two brothers.[24]

Chaldeans have been known to give up promising careers in other fields in order to help run the store of an elderly father or uncle, or to

Many Chaldean stores are co-owned by relatives. Here Patrick Najor and his father, Emmanuel, are pictured in their store, Bayshore Market, which they formerly owned in New Baltimore, Michigan. (Photo courtesy of Dr. Michelle Najor.)

open a store in order to assist relatives in immigrating. In some instances, the family as a whole, rather than an individual, owns the business or other property. This can be confusing to outsiders who marry into the community, as with one American woman, engaged to a Chaldean man, who wondered which of the family's several cars might belong to her and her fiancé once they were married.

There is a negative side to this assistance, however. Obviously there is a quid pro quo involved: If extended families help their members in need, they also expect these same members to return the favor when other members are in need. This can lead to considerable demands placed on the members. Extended family members usually expect to be included in all of their family members' undertakings and decisions as well.

Socializing among extended family members is also a constant activity. Chaldeans are more likely to socialize with other Chaldeans, and community and church gatherings are frequently used as opportunities to bring the extended family together. This is especially true of immigrants and those with limited command of English, who depend upon others from their background and language group for social contact. However, even American-born Chaldeans report that their closest friends are Chaldean. Interestingly, many of them do not view these as "ethnic" ties, but simply as "doing things with the people I grew up with and know the best." That they are all Chaldean seems to them to be an accidental part of the picture. For them, the Chaldean community largely consists of their extended family relationships.

A major area of concern in most extended family systems is the choice of a spouse. Obviously the close-knit family network described here cannot operate effectively if the members are not compatible. If a child marries a non-Chaldean, or even someone from within the community with whom the family does not get along, the intricate network of cooperation, socializing, and business ventures might be difficult to maintain. Consequently, as with many ethnic groups, most Chaldean families strongly prefer that their children marry others of the same ethnic background.

Young Chaldeans, even from the second or third generation, recognize this, and some openly admit that they would consider their parents' wishes in choosing a spouse. There is no question, however, that the incidence of intermarriage is increasing. The *2000–2001 Chaldean Directory* lists twenty-eight persons under non-Chaldean names, indicating Chaldean women who are married to non-Chaldean men, and, hence, no longer have Chaldean surnames. Undoubtedly, there are also many Chaldean males who have married non-Chaldeans, but this cannot be observed from the *Directory* listing, since the maiden name of the non-Chaldean spouse does not appear.

The fact that these people continue to be listed in the *Directory* illustrates the fact that Chaldeans who marry non-Chaldeans are still recognized as part of the Chaldean community. Most often these non-Chaldeans are Roman Catholic, and the marriages typically take place in the Chaldean Church. Many of these Chaldeans (and sometimes their non-Chaldean spouses as well) are active in various Chaldean community activities and organizations. As one non-Chaldean man, married to a Chaldean woman, once told me, "We knew we would have the most trouble with her family, so we decided to do things the way they wanted it." Following the marriage, contact with the Chaldean extended family on the part of the intermarried couple tends to remain high. Some non-Chaldean spouses, for example, are in business with relatives of their Chaldean spouses. There are no data, however, to indicate whether the rate of extended family contact currently remains as high with exogamous as with endogamous marriages.

Direct choice of a child's spouse by his or her parents is rare in the community today. Indeed, it was not common for most of the latter part of the twentieth century. Parental influence is more likely to be more informal. Parents can make it easy for their children to date an "approved" person, by providing for social gatherings, making cars available, and so on. If they disapprove, they simply do not provide such assistance. Such informal influence can be so successful that the young couple is not even aware it has occurred.

The American tradition of "dating" before marriage has been a matter of debate in the Chaldean community for some time. In Chaldean families that are long established in the United States, dating is fairly accepted. There is a greater degree of debate among those more recently arrived. At the same time, however, traditions in the country of origin have also changed, and American-born children of immigrants sometimes complain that their immigrant cousins have more freedom than they do to date and choose a spouse. It should also be recognized that the inclusion of parental preference in the choice of one's spouse does not simply extend to choosing a Chaldean versus an outsider. This is a very large community at this point. Instances of "inappropriate" choices even within the Chaldean community are not unknown. Family reputation and past relations between the two families are likely to come into play in influencing their children's choices.

The extreme emphasis on the extended family should not be construed as a diminution of the importance of the nuclear unit of husband, wife, and children, however. In some ethnic groups it has been noted that social gatherings tend to separate into gender-based subgroups.[25] In the past, such a gender separation occurred among Chaldeans. Until the mid-twentieth century, for example, Chaldean church services had men and women sitting in separate sections of the church. Today, however, husband and wife generally attend community and extended family activities as a unit. Once established, Chaldean marriages tend to be lasting. While more common today than in the past, divorce among Chaldeans is still unusual. This may largely be a holdover from the old arranged marriage system, in which the marriage was seen as a lifelong bond, not to be dissolved when the initial romantic glow disappeared.

The mother, in particular, occupies a preeminent role in the individual family unit. Traditional Chaldean families were largely gender segregated, and men typically were not involved in household activities or care of their young children. This, too, is changing today. . Some Chaldean women now work outside the home, many in highly skilled or professional positions, and many in their extended family's economic ventures. However, the status of the mother as the central focus of the home remains. While feminists may see this as a controlling influence on women's power, this approach often fails to recognize the considerable power of this position. A mother's decisions concerning home-related matters are rarely questioned by her husband.

To summarize, it is difficult to overstate the importance of the Chaldean family. Chaldean marriages are enduring, with divorce less likely than in American society as a whole. Chaldean family ties extend beyond the bonds of husband, wife, and children to include a wide variety of other relatives. Individuals have strong ties to these other relatives, even extending across national boundaries to the old country or other Chaldean communities in the United States. Individuals can expect assistance from these kin in times of need, and conversely, have responsibilities to them when they are in need. Chaldeans do not generally live in extended family households, but may include such persons within the household when the need arises.

Along with the church, the extended family is one of the two most important institutions in the Chaldean community. It is of such importance that outsiders sometimes view it as the major dimension of Chaldean life and culture. For many second- and subsequent-generation Chaldeans, the family remains their most important, perhaps their only, tie to the Chaldean community. While they have long since ceased to attend services at the Chaldean Church, they remain close to the extended family. Indeed, for many Chaldeans, the extended family *is* the community.

The Chaldean Church

Although Chaldeans are immigrants from Iraq, they are not typical Iraqis, the major distinguishing factor being their Christian religion. Christians as a whole make up only about 6 percent of the Iraqi population.[26] The region in which Telkaif is located has been home to many varieties of Christians (including Protestants, Eastern Orthodox, and Roman Catholics) almost since the beginning of the Christian era. The earliest Chaldean immigrants came to the United States before the establishment of Iraq as a separate nation and the development of Arab nationalism. Consequently, the Chaldean community was established on the basis of the more narrow identification with the original village and religion, rather than the national identity of Iraq. Although almost all recent immigrants speak Arabic, identification with the Chaldean religion and language remains strong, even among those who no longer speak the ancestral language. Many Chaldeans still do not identify primarily with Iraq or the Arab movement, which tends to be associated with the Muslim religion in the minds of Christians and Muslims alike. Indeed, the discomfort they felt living in a predominantly Muslim world is often mentioned by Chaldeans as a major impetus for emigrating.[27]

Historical Importance of the Chaldean Religion

Consequently, religion remains a major component of the Chaldean community. Residents of Telkaif are members of a specific rite, or division, of the Roman Catholic Church. This rite is called the Chaldean rite, from which comes the name by which the community is identified. The Christians from this area of northern Iraq claim to be an "apostolic church"—dating their Christian heritage from the earliest days of the Christian era. Chaldeans say they were converted to Christianity by the apostle Thomas, together with his disciple, St. Addai, in the first century after the life and death of Jesus.[28] St. Addai is also said to have written the prayers used in the Chaldean version of the Mass. Another tradition holds that the three kings who visited Jesus shortly after his birth were from among their people.

The Middle East has been a crossroads between East and West since before the Christian era. Long before the birth of Christ, Babylonians, Assyrians, Sumerians, Greeks, and Hebrews all lived in the area. They were followed by many varieties of Christians as well as by Muslim Arabs. The area today is still populated by many groups who claim descent from one or more of these groups. The original Christians from this area call themselves the "Assyrian Church of the East," based on their claim of descent from the ancient Assyrian Empire that once occupied this territory, as well as their alleged tie to the language of ancient Assyria.[29]

Assyrian Christians have experienced many of the same divisions that have characterized Christianity throughout the world. One of the early bishops from this area was Nestorius. In the fifth century, A.D., Nestorius differed from the Church of the West on some points of theology, specifically, whether the Son of God, when he became man, brought his divine identity with him.[30] In short, the question was whether Jesus was both God and man at the same time, or only man. The Western Catholic Church believed that Christ was both God and man; Nestorius supposedly believed that Christ was only man.

This has particular implications for Mary, the mother of Jesus. The Western Church claimed she could rightfully be called "Mother of God." Nestorius's position, on the other hand, would accord her only the title "Mother of Christ." Nestorius was proclaimed a heretic by the pope and the Roman Catholic Church in the fifth century, leading to a long separation between the eastern and western Christian churches. Relations between the Assyrian and Roman churches have varied over the centuries, at times leading to reunification.

One such unification occurred in 1553, when relations between Assyrian Christians and Rome warmed to the point that Pope Julius accepted the bishop of Mosul into union with Rome, and gave him the title of "Patriarch of the Chaldeans." Thus was born the "Chaldean Rite" of the Roman Catholic Church.[31] In Roman Catholic tradition, a "rite" is a specific division of the Catholic Church that is accorded a certain degree of autonomy and permitted to maintain its own set of rituals and leadership. A patriarch is the leader of such a rite. The title "Chaldean" was given to the rite to denote their association with the ancient tribal groups of Mesopotamia. Chaldeans occupied Mesopotamia as well as modern Syria beginning in about 900 B.C. Chaldeans ruled the area from their major city, Babylon, until they were conquered by the Persians under Cyrus in 539 B.C. Ancient Chaldeans spoke Aramaic, a modern version of which is spoken by Assyrian and Chaldean Christians today.

Not all Christians joined with Rome at that time, however. Over the centuries, various groups have joined with Rome and split away again, some several times. The town of Telkaif dates its unification with Rome to about 1830, when another bishop of Mosul, John IX Hormizd, joined with Rome and was given the title of Patriarch of Mosul. Some early residents of the Detroit community recalled hearing their grandparents describe the religious controversies—some involving actual physical conflicts—that occurred in Telkaif at that time.

Chaldean Christians Today

Assyrian Christians from northern Iraq have also joined with other Christian denominations over the centuries, including Eastern Orthodox Churches and various Protestant denominations during the era of European colonialism in the Middle East. Some Assyrian groups have attempted to unite these different religious groups together into a common cultural group, recognizing their common language and historical origins. One such unifying organization publishes the magazine *Neneveh,* to help draw these groups together and downplay their religious differences.[32]

In November 1994, relations between the Assyrian Church of the East and the Roman Catholic Church warmed considerably with a meeting in Rome between Mar Dinkha IV, Patriarch of the Assyrian Church, and Pope John Paul II. They declared their common belief in Jesus Christ as both God and man, and the right of the Virgin Mary to the title of Mother of God, repudiated the earlier doctrinal controversy, which they attributed to a misunderstanding, and expressed a hope for eventual unification.

At present, however, Chaldeans and Assyrians from other religious preferences tend to remain separate. The town of Turlock in northern California is an example of a community in which Assyrians from both Protestant and Roman Catholic backgrounds have operated as a single community for some time. This may, in part, be due to the relative size of the communities. Turlock's Assyrians are much fewer in number and must include Assyrians from different religious backgrounds to remain operative. Detroit's Chaldean population has more than enough members to operate as a single community.

The Chaldean Church in Detroit

The Chaldean religion plays an extremely important role in the community. Chaldeans tend to be very devout, with the church serving as the center of the community on many occasions. Chaldeans are anxious to have others recognize them as Catholic. In the past this has not been an easy task. Because their services and customs differ greatly from those of the majority of Catholics, they are often assumed to be Eastern Orthodox. They may be viewed suspiciously by other Catholics, even, at times, by Catholic priests. When I first began to study the community, one priest told me he didn't know much about them, but commented that they were "probably Orthodox." As the community's size has made it more visible, more people are aware of its Roman Catholic connection.

That others might not associate Chaldeans with the Catholic Church is not surprising in view of the numerous variations from traditional Roman Catholic patterns. In terms of basic doctrine, Chaldean beliefs and moral traditions are identical with those of other Catholics. Both accept the pope of Rome as the head of the Church. However, the rituals of the Chaldean rite differ considerably from those of the more commonly known Western or "Latin Rite" (so called because it formerly used Latin as the language for the major prayer, the Mass). These differences were particularly strong in the country of origin, and could be seen in the early churches in Detroit. In recent years, however, a modernizing or Westernizing influence has been operating, not only in the United States, but reportedly in Iraq as well.

An example of these changes is the altered structure of the church building. Chaldean churches formerly had a wall between the altar and the people, with the altar area reserved for the priest and other ministers. Churches were also divided into separate sections for men and women. In the mid-twentieth century, many members of the congregation still preferred to sit in gender-segregated areas. Today, however, these patterns have largely disappeared, and Chaldean churches in Detroit could easily pass for any other Catholic church. Perhaps the major remnant in the church buildings from the Chaldeans' Eastern heritage is the use of some historic Eastern-style decorations. Chaldean churches, for example, are more likely to use a dome. One church (Sacred Heart) has a façade modeled after the gates of the ancient city of Babylon, in honor of the community's Babylonian heritage.

The most dramatic differences between the Chaldean and Latin Rite churches remain in the area of church rituals and services, the Aramaic language being the most obvious difference. Chaldeans proudly claim that they pray in the language used by Jesus and some of the New Testament writers.[33] It should be noted, however, that there is considerable difference between the language of the Chaldean rituals and the language that Chaldeans used in their daily life. Here, too, is a major area of change in the church in recent years, since recent immigrants do not know Chaldean, and many church services are now recited in Arabic, much as the use of Latin by Western churches has been replaced by English or other vernacular languages.

Other differences between the Chaldean and Western rites involve music, clerical patterns, baptism, and marriage. In the traditional Chaldean rituals, only the human voice and rhythm instruments were used; today, organ music has been introduced. The Chaldean Rite also formerly had a married clergy; today's Chaldean clergy, like the Western rite clergy, are celibate. The form of baptism for new members is also a ritual pattern currently undergoing change. Most Western Catholic churches baptize by means of pouring water over the head. Chaldeans traditionally have used the method of immersing the candidate in a pool of water, a pattern that is retained in the Chaldean community and has become the pattern in many Western Catholic churches as well. Marriages in Telkaif and other northern Iraqi villages were traditionally held in the bride's home. Today Chaldean marriages take place in the church; but for the language, they resemble any other Catholic marriage.

While the earliest Chaldeans came to Detroit in the first decade of the twentieth century, the first Chaldean Church was not founded until after the Second World War. This is not surprising, even for a highly religious community like the Chaldeans. The earliest years of any immigrant community are largely concentrated on adaptation to the new homeland and earning a living. It is also necessary to attain a critical mass of members before community institutions can be established. By the 1930s, the Chaldean community had a sufficient number of members (approximately 120) to establish a church; however, World War II intervened, making immigration more difficult.

During this period, Chaldeans attended other Catholic churches in the area, and most sent their children to Catholic schools. Most were Western rite churches, but the services of Western rite Catholic churches used Latin rather than Aramaic. Furthermore, these churches were largely under the influence of other ethnic groups, such as the Irish, the Italians, and the Poles. Hence their ethnic customs, as well as their church services, were somewhat alien. There was a particular preference for another eastern rite Catholic church, St. Maron's, which served Detroit's Lebanese community. St. Maron's was part of the "Maronite rite," used the Arabic language, and had rituals that were somewhat similar to the Chaldean rite. Use of St. Maron's was particularly important for special services, such as marriages, baptisms, and funerals.

In the mid 1940s, Chaldean leaders sought the assistance of the Catholic archbishop of Detroit, the late Edward Cardinal Mooney, and the Iraqi Patriarch of the Chaldean rite in obtaining a Chaldean priest. Rev. Thomas Rauphael Bidawid came to Detroit in 1947, initially using the facilities of other Catholic churches to offer Chaldean services. The first Chaldean church building was dedicated in 1948 and given the name "Mother of God," clearly identifying its Roman Catholic affiliation. Mother of God Church has been relocated several times, as the Chaldean population has moved, from the central Detroit and Highland Park area in the 1930–1960 period to the northwestern suburbs during the latter half of the twentieth century. The church is now

Rev. Thomas Bidawid was the first priest to serve the Chaldean community in Detroit. He founded the first Chaldean parish, Mother of God Church, in 1947. He later returned to the Middle East and was made a bishop of the Chaldean Rite, serving until his death in 1971. (Photo from the Chaldean Community Directory, 2000–2001.)

located in the city of Southfield, on Berg Road near Ten Mile Road. In 1982, Mar Ibrahim Ibrahim was appointed pastor of Mother of God, and bishop of the newly created St. Thomas the Apostle Chaldean Catholic Diocese in the United States. The church has now been elevated to the status of a "cathedral," indicating its function as a bishop's church. While still using the name Mother of God, the church is also called the Cathedral of Our Lady of Chaldeans.

A second Chaldean church, Sacred Heart, was founded in 1973 by Rev. Jacob Yasso. It is located on Seven Mile Road near John R Street in Detroit. This church is named after one of the two churches in the Chaldeans' original town of Telkaif. As noted earlier, the Babylonian facade of Sacred Heart Church pays tribute to the Chaldean community's roots in this ancient culture. This church has served for years as an entry point into the United States for Chaldean families. Four additional churches have since been founded to serve the more dispersed community: Mar Addai parish, on Coolidge Highway in Oak Park, founded in 1979; St. Joseph parish, on Big Beaver Road in Troy, founded

The interior of most Chaldean churches closely resembles that of other Roman Catholic churches in the Detroit area. This is the main altar of Sacred Heart Chaldean Church in Detroit. Sacred Heart was the second Chaldean parish established in the Detroit area, and is currently the oldest of the Chaldean church buildings.

in 1981; and St. Thomas, on Maple Road in West Bloomfield, established in 1994. St. George Chaldean Church, located in Shelby Township, is scheduled to open in late 2004, to serve the growing Chaldean population in Macomb County, in the northeast section of the Detroit Metropolitan Area. There are also five Chaldean parishes in California, two in Chicago, and one in Scottsdale, Arizona, and a second Chaldean diocese was established in California in 2002.

With six Chaldean churches, it is now more convenient for Chaldeans in the Detroit area to attend services of their own rite, but there is no church requirement that they do so. In theory, they should use their own rite for important rituals (marriage, baptism, or funerals). However, many Chaldeans, particularly those of the third, fourth, or later generations who were educated in the United States, generally attend the most convenient church. This pattern intensified in the last quarter of the twentieth century, as western Catholic churches held services in English rather than in Latin, while Chaldean services remained in the very unfamiliar Aramaic.

Some Chaldean churches have adapted to the needs of their diverse population by altering the character of the services. Services may be held in English for American-born Chaldeans. Many services are held in Arabic, to accommodate newcomers from Iraq. There is still a strong commitment in the community, however, to the Aramaic language, and some churches have introduced Aramaic language classes and developed educational materials to familiarize their members with the traditional language of the Chaldean Church.[34]

The Chaldean Church as a Social Focus for the Community

Even for those Chaldeans who rarely attend Chaldean services, the Chaldean Church remains an important focus of life in a number of respects. First of all, it is an important focus of community identity. Chaldeans are aware that their religious group is unique—an Eastern religion with a Western connection as well as a historic tie both to Christ and His apostles and to ancient Babylon. Even Americanized Chaldeans express pride in this heritage.

Second, the Chaldean Church remains an important focus for the social events of the community. Important milestones and events in the life of the community and the extended family are celebrated in the church. Even nonreligious Chaldeans come to the Chaldean Church for the weddings, funerals, baptisms, and first communions of relatives. Holidays, such as Christmas and Easter, and memorial masses on the anniversary of a relative's death, also draw people to the Chaldean Church. Chaldean Church services are not simply religious ceremonies; they are also social events. Hence they draw in not only observant Chaldeans, but also those who attend primarily to see relatives and friends. This social character, in itself, can be a deterrent for some people, who complain that the church has lost its character as a place of prayer and become primarily a social gathering.

The Chaldean Church serves as a gathering place in a broader sense as well, in that many community organizations have their base of operations in one or another of the churches. Women's groups, youth groups, businessmen's associations—all tend to meet in one of the Chaldean churches. The number of community organizations has increased to the point that a "Chaldean Federation," encompassing all

Receiving First Communion in the Catholic Church usually occurs at seven or eight years of age and is a major event in the lives of Chaldean children. Families often arrange for two or more siblings or cousins to celebrate together, and host a party similar to a wedding reception, with the children dressed as miniature brides and grooms. Here cousins Grace Lutfy and Emmanuel Najor examine the cake for their joint First Communion. (Photo courtesy of Dr. Michelle Najor.)

of the Chaldean-related groups, now exists. Even nonreligious Chaldeans, or those who may have transferred their religious affiliation to the dominant Catholic rite or to another religious group, are drawn to the Chaldean Church for such activities.

Chaldean churches also serve as an educational center. This educational function is a multifaceted operation. On the one hand, it has long been recognized that immigrant organizations provide an acculturation service for members of an ethnic group. The ethnic community and its organizations provide a situation in which new arrivals find

Founding Members of the Detroit Chaldean Community. Several founding members of the Detroit Chaldean community met to greet their founding pastor when he visited Detroit after being named a bishop. Pictured are: Rev. Jacob Yasso, Tom Denha and son, Zia Gabbara, Sam Dabish, Mrs. Katrina Dabish, Bishop Thomas Bidawid, Mrs. Susan Essa, Mrs. Habeeba Hesano, Mrs. Miriam Nany, Mrs. Barbara Hakim, Tom Matti, and Thomas Hakim. (Photo published with permission of Michigan History.*)*

familiar faces and cultural patterns—people who share their values and attitudes and know their language. Since many recent arrivals know Arabic rather than Aramaic (Chaldean), Chaldean churches now offer assistance in both languages.

Recent arrivals can also find assistance in the church in adapting to their new environment: help to learn the English language, contacts for getting a job or starting a business, information about places to live, help with immigration problems, and many other types of assistance. Chaldean organizations, particularly the churches, have long provided such assistance. As with many other ethnic groups, Chaldean religious leaders have often provided assistance to community members that has gone far beyond simply training in religion. Like the priests, ministers, and rabbis of other ethnic groups that preceded them, Chaldean religious leaders have often provided their parishioners with assistance with secular problems as well.

Chaldean community and church organizations provide an opportunity for community members to learn about and retain their heritage. They provide language instruction in Arabic and Aramaic, and information about the historical origins of the Chaldean people. Education in the Chaldean version of the Catholic religion is offered for children and adults alike. Religious education for the children has become particularly important in recent decades, after the closure of many Roman Catholic schools. In many respects, the decrease in Catholic schools has forced Chaldean parents to teach Chaldean rite Catholicism to their children, rather than the dominant rite, and has forced Chaldean churches to provide this training.

It is clear, however, that the Chaldean churches are losing contact with second-, third-, and fourth-generation Chaldeans, who prefer the more "modern," Americanized services of other Catholic Churches—or even of other religions or no religion at all. The remaining ties of these community members to the Chaldean Church are primarily through their families, and they may attend only for family-related gatherings such as weddings or funerals. Even immigrants today have an altered relation to the church, as there are more and more educated professionals who speak their language and can provide the nonreligious services formerly provided by the churches. With the increased professionalization of society, as well as of the ethnic community, ethnic churches no longer serve as the multifaceted resource centers they once did. Other institutions have developed to take over their nonreligious functions, including Arabic- and Chaldean-language newspapers and radio and TV broadcasts, private Chaldean social clubs, secular education programs, social service agencies, and so on. Immigrants still require these services, but the ethnic church is no longer their primary source for assistance.

Perhaps the major influence the Chaldean Church retains in the Chaldean community today is its strong sense of communal identity for Detroit Chaldeans. This is true even of Chaldeans with relatively weak ties to the Chaldean Church and few ethnic connections other than family. Many still express pride in their heritage, and a strong consciousness of its unique character. In particular, this can be seen in the reluctance of most Chaldeans to identify and associate with other groups from the Arabic-speaking Middle East. With a few notable exceptions, Chaldeans, even those born and reared in the United States, are quick to point out the religious differences between themselves and other Arabs and Iraqis, whom they associate with the Muslim religion. This will become the topic of discussion in a subsequent section.

The Chaldean Grocery Store

It may seem strange to list the mundane grocery store on an equal footing with church and family in the delineation of Chaldean community institutions. After all, religious and familial institutions are generally considered to be of higher cultural value than crass means of making a living. This parallel position is accurate, however, and probably not unusual in the description of ethnic community institutions. Nothing takes priority in the life of a new immigrant over finding a means of making a living. Until this has been accomplished, there is little room for anything else, even religion and family. Hence the means by which members of an ethnic community make a living is highly deserving of serious analysis. For the Chaldean community, the primary economic institution has been the grocery store.

Economic activities have generally been viewed as the aspect of life in which a member of an ethnic community is most likely to encounter persons from other groups. Family, church (or synagogue or mosque), and social groups are usually limited to members of an immigrant's own ethnic background, and often constitute the most important components of his or her life. In the economy, however, it is usually assumed that members of an ethnic group will encounter outsiders at an early point after their arrival in a new country, and that these will continue to be the most frequent encounters an immigrant will have with outsiders. Furthermore, most observers assume that members of immigrant communities will participate in the activities of the overall economy, and will eventually achieve acceptance and move up the economic ladder. While it is recognized that major discrimination and prejudice on the part of society toward a specific group, such as blacks, can delay this process considerably, it is generally assumed that most white immigrant groups fit this model.[35]

The Grocery Store as an Example of an Ethnic Occupation

This picture of participation in the broader economic sphere does not apply to many immigrant groups. While some Chaldeans have followed this pattern, the Chaldean community as a whole has not. Social scientists are increasingly aware that many ethnic communities use the economic sphere as another area in which the ethnic community can work together as effectively as in family, religious, and social life. Jewish merchants in New York in the first half of the twentieth century are an obvious example, as are Italians in the construction industry and Chinese in the laundry and restaurant businesses. More recently, Koreans and other Asian store owners are also examples.[36]

From its earliest years in the Detroit area, the Chaldean community has occupied such a niche through its association with the retail grocery business. While it is not totally clear how Chaldeans became associated with the grocery trade, there is evidence that Lebanese Maronite Christians who preceded them to the Detroit area had also owned grocery stores. Since the groups were of similar religion and origin in the Middle East, the Lebanese may have introduced Chaldeans to the grocery trade.

As early as 1917, the *City Directory for Detroit* listed a grocery store owned by members of the Chaldean community (George Najor and Thomas Kory). By 1923, less than two decades after the first Chaldean arrived in Detroit, there were 4 Chaldean-owned grocery stores. By 1962, the number had grown to 120 stores, and more than half of the nuclear families in the community made their living primarily from the grocery business or associated enterprises. By the early 1990s, the Associated Food Dealers of Metropolitan Detroit estimated that there were over 1,000 Chaldean-owned food stores.

The earliest stores were typically single-owner, "Mom and Pop"–type enterprises. They were owned and operated primarily by a man and his wife. They had no employees other than their children, and they worked from early morning to late night. Children, both boys and girls, began working in the store at a very early age. The stores were small and carried a limited line of products. Many emphasized personal service, however, as they were willing to grant credit, deliver to the home, and often special order specific products for individual customers.[37]

As their ventures prospered, Chaldeans moved into larger stores with more employees, a wider range of products, and often with more partners in a single store. Some of the larger stores also employed persons outside the Chaldean community. Chaldeans also moved into other ventures closely associated with the grocery business. The wholesale grocery supply business, providing canned goods, snack foods, milk products, and sundries to the retail stores, is an obvious example. Others provided services needed in the business, such as alarm systems, linen supplies, commercial real estate assistance, and so on. Many Chaldean immigrants also gained employment in wholesale grocery enterprises owned by non-Chaldeans—on the assumption that they could gain clients through their Chaldean community contacts. Business loans through sources internal to the community were also common.

Expanding into Other Economic Opportunities

In the last quarter of the twentieth century, the food industry changed a great deal, as it was largely taken over by the giant chains, leaving little room for the independent grocery store owner. The smaller stores have largely been replaced by "party stores" or "convenience stores," offering an even more limited range of products but focusing on beer, wine, and liquor; often such small outlets are also associated with a gas station. Increasingly, other Middle Eastern groups, such as the Lebanese or the Syrians, have taken over such gas station/convenience stores as well.

The grocery business and its associated industries have been a great aid to Chaldeans in assisting with immigration to the United States. The financial strain involved in bringing relatives to this country is alleviated considerably by a family economic enterprise. Newcomers can be put to work almost immediately in the family grocery store, performing such simple tasks as sweeping floors, stocking shelves, and the like. As their use of the English language improves, they may also run the cash register, assist customers, and so on. This entrepreneurial business pattern has characterized most ethnic occupations, all of which share a number of traits. They include a number of relatively unskilled jobs, which can be easily learned by a newcomer.

Many Chaldean stores also serve as outlets for the Michigan Lottery. In this picture, Michael Jones proudly displays his lottery winnings to Adnan Najor, owner of Midtown Liquor and Deli in downtown Detroit.

They require little awareness of the dominant American culture and can be performed with little skill in the English language. Although they can become quite large and elaborate, most require a relatively small investment at the outset, when immigrants have little to invest. They also allow a considerable period of time in which an immigrant can earn a living without extensive contact with persons outside of his or her familiar group. Hence the immigrant has the luxury of interacting primarily with members of his or her own group during the initial period of becoming accustomed to American society. This pattern has served many immigrant groups well for more than a century.

Functions of an Ethnic Occupation

An ethnic occupation therefore performs a number of functions for an ethnic community. These functions can be both positive and negative. Perhaps the most obvious positive function is the financial benefit. It enables the community to provide financial support to newcomers in their difficult early years in this country. Indeed, the Chaldean community is recognized throughout the Detroit area as having achieved economic success in the grocery business, and some have become quite wealthy. This can be a drawback, however, to those Chaldeans who are not so successful, since most Detroit-area citizens assume that all Chaldeans are very rich and do not need any help!

There are some additional impacts of the grocery business on the Chaldean community. These may be more subtle but they are also very real. Since it is the business by which the majority of the members of the Chaldean community make their living, the entire community is very closely tied to the grocery trade. The strong business connections provide an additional means by which family ties are cemented. Many stores and other grocery-related ventures are partnerships of fathers and sons, brothers or brothers-in-law, uncles and nephews.[38] Joint ventures provide greater capital, in addition to easing the workload. In the earliest years, most partnerships were primarily male ventures. Traditionally, women were usually involved only as employees, to "help out" when needed. Increasingly, however, women may also be involved in family economic activities.

The assistance that businesses provide for new immigrants takes many forms. Not only do new immigrants have a job waiting for them, they also may receive assistance in the immigration process itself. Under immigration law, immigrants into the United States must prove that they will have a job on their arrival. An ethnic business can help to insure this. They operate in a similar manner to the Italian "padrones," who helped to place new immigrants on construction jobs. While they are sometimes accused of exploiting new immigrants, paying low wages and exacting long hours, they also provide an essential service for new immigrants with little skill and in need of financial support. Chaldeans are well aware that the grocery business serves the function of assisting immigration. Indeed, some community members specifically state that they left other jobs to open a store because they had relatives who wanted to immigrate. Those in the community who do not own their own business must support newly arrived family members, who represent a drain on their income. Those who own their own stores, however, can put newcomers to work immediately to help out.

Even after a family is fairly well situated, the grocery business represents an important focus. Many Chaldeans give family-related

Chaldean stores are operations that involve the entire family, with children often spending time in their parents' store. Here Joey and Emmanuel Najor enjoy a snack in the store owned by their father and grandfather, Patrick and Emmanuel Najor Sr. (Photo courtesy of Dr. Michelle Najor.)

reasons for remaining in the grocery business. They say their father or an uncle or brother needed help in the store, or they like the opportunity to work with relatives. The common occupation also provides an additional focus of interest for the community. Community activities are often scheduled to accommodate the extended hours of store owners, and grocery-related talk is very common at community gatherings, often making the nongrocer feel somewhat left out.

There is also ample evidence that ethnic occupations perform a valuable function for the wider society as a whole. Perhaps the most obvious is the fact that it helps to insure that new arrivals will not become a drain on the society at large in the early years after their arrival—an issue that has been a major concern in the United States since the arrival of the great waves of immigrants over a century ago.

Indeed, this was one of the concerns that lead to the development of the quota limits on immigration.[39] Ethnic economic structures also provide an opportunity for newcomers to learn aspects of American culture in relatively easy stages. With the grocery business in particular, it is also obvious that new Chaldean immigrants receive an early introduction to American entrepreneurial concepts and values. Many immigrants recall learning English by reading the labels on cans in the stores.

At the same time, an ethnic occupation is not an unmixed blessing. Chaldean success in the grocery business has created considerable resentment on the part of others in the community. It has also been suggested that some ethnic groups deliberately situate their businesses in less favorable areas of the community. In this way, they may serve as "middle men," mediating between the poor and the powerful business interests, most of whom prefer not to associate with persons of lower status. Jewish businesses in the early twentieth century, and Asian businesses in more recent years, are examples of this. In the same manner, Chaldean grocery stores have often provided grocery services in low-income, black areas of the city, which the major grocery chains have neglected to a considerable extent.[40] This pattern tends to generate resentment on the part of the lower-income customers they serve, and interethnic conflict has occasionally flared up between African-American customers and Chaldean business owners.

Even within the Chaldean community, the ethnic business provides a source of strain as well as cohesion. Members of the community often become highly competitive, pitting individual store owners against one another and causing rifts between families. Detroit-area residents often assume that the Chaldeans have a highly developed grocery store coalition—a sort of Chaldean grocery store chain. However, most Chaldean stores are independent operations, and numerous attempts to develop alliances over the years have been unsuccessful.

Instead, there is a great deal of competition between Chaldean businesses. Many stores are located near each other, and compete for the same customers, a competition that has become fierce at times. Some of these recreate family rivalries that were brought with them from Iraq, where economic success and affluence was also prized. In the United States, a prime way of displaying one's success is through the size and appearance of one's store. Furthermore, Chaldeans who have assisted newcomers in becoming established generally expect a return on their investment at a later point. .

A major dysfunction of the ethnic occupation is the impact it has on community members who are not part of the dominant occupation. The number of Chaldean doctors, dentists, lawyers, and engineers is constantly growing. Yet community activities and conversations continue to focus on the grocery business, isolating persons in other fields. In some instances this isolation can lead these members to become less involved in the community or to leave it altogether. However, this also suggests that another consequence of an ethnic occupation is its impact on assimilation into the wider society. As I noted at the outset of this section, the economic sphere has traditionally been the arena in which members of an ethnic group have come into contact with others from outside the group. With an ethnic occupation, contact in this important sphere is more limited.

In general, then, assimilation into American society as a whole tends to be more rapid for those who are not involved in the Chaldean grocery business, while the grocery business acts as an "insulator" against assimilation for those involved in it. Indeed, some Chaldeans have indicated that they selected an occupation other than the grocery business as a means of limiting their contact with the community. Nongrocers who would like to remain part of the community, however, may feel like outcasts at times. It is likely that other ethnic communities with a shared occupation have had similar experiences.

Another dysfunction of an ethnic occupation is that it may arrest the assimilation process at a fairly early point, which can be a problem both for members of the ethnic group and for society as a whole. By allowing immigrants to limit their contacts outside the ethnic community, an ethnic occupation may delay their long-term adjustment to the wider society, inhibiting their chances for advancement and allowing for the persistence of numerous relatively autonomous subcommunities in society as a whole. It is, of course, debatable whether or not this is dysfunctional. If the goal is assimilation into the wider society, it is; if, on the other hand, the goal is the advancement of the group as a whole, it is clearly not. However, from the standpoint of individual advancement, the short-term function of aiding in adjustment may actually delay adjustment to the broader society in the long term.

In summary, the grocery business has played a major role in the development of the Chaldean community in the Detroit area. Without it, the community could never have progressed to the degree it has. It serves not only as the major means of making a living, but as a means of uniting families, and the focus of numerous community activities. It is one of the mechanisms for drawing the entire community together. With the church and the extended family, it is part of the three-way institutional structure of the community. An understanding of this economic institution is as crucial to an analysis of the Chaldean community as the study of its family structure and religion.

A Changing Population

Our discussion to this point has focused on general background information on the Chaldean community, as well as basic cultural patterns and the major social institutions that hold the community together. However, any community is a dynamic force, constantly adapting to its surroundings. Nowhere is this more true than in an ethnic community. New themes are coming into play in the Chaldean community as it moves into its second century in the Detroit area. The nature of the Chaldean population has changed significantly, and Chaldean conceptions of their community and its identity have also been altered in response to local and world affairs. Analysis of these changing patterns will be the focus of the next two sections.

Coping with Growth, New Immigrants, and Aging

In the last quarter of the twentieth century, the Chaldean community faced new problems. One might accurately say that this community had "growing pains." In the early 1970s, community records listed only about ten to fifteen thousand members. By the mid-1990s, the same records listed about sixty-five thousand members, and community leaders claimed that ten thousand or more had probably been missed.[41]

As it moves into the twenty-first century, the community has become a highly diverse population, counting among its members immigrants remaining from the early waves of Chaldean migration; their children and grandchildren; and many, many immigrants who have come in the last quarter of the twentieth century, not to mention a continuing flow of new immigrants each year, many of them refugees from a war-torn homeland. These factors combine to create a complex set of problems. To achieve its goals, the Chaldean community must deal with the needs and demands of many different kinds of members at the same time.

In the early years of development of any ethnic community, institutions tend to center around the practical daily necessities of recent immigrants trying to adjust to American society: establishing a means of economic support; finding a home; learning the English language; and so on. Ethnic community institutions develop to assist new immigrants with these problems, and the successful ethnic community is one that can provide these types of assistance. This was the nature of the Chaldean community in the first half of the twentieth century. It became fairly well established as a mechanism for providing this type of assistance to a reasonable number of new immigrants on an annual basis.

Once they can provide for the necessities of life, however, community members have the leisure to think about providing for their social and cultural interests. In this period, they become more focused on the values of the society and culture they left behind. They now have the luxury of focusing on those aspects of old country culture that they miss: their unique religious, historical, and family traditions; reproducing cultural artifacts and language; and so on. This pattern has characterized nearly all American ethnic groups, from the original English settlers who founded our Anglo-centered society, culture, and government, to the myriad of ethnic communities—German, Irish, Italian, African-American, Polish, Greek, Jewish, Mexican, Asian, to name but a few—that followed them. All sought to reproduce their unique traditions in their new home, and to transmit these traditions to their children and grandchildren in perpetuity. The establishment of the first Chaldean church in the United States in the 1940s was early evidence of this later stage of development for the Chaldean community.

Like other groups, ethnic communities often find that their members' needs change as they grow older. It has been noted that members of different ethnic groups experience aging in different ways.[42] In the past, with shorter life spans, most ethnic communities did not have to deal with such problems, since few of their members reached an advanced age, and families could usually deal with these few cases. Today, however, ethnic communities are discovering that they must deal with an increasingly older population. After the first few decades of its existence, an ethnic community is no longer a group of young immigrants who need assistance in adapting to their new homeland. Neither is it a fairly well established community of immigrants, coping with the problems of rearing children according to traditional values in a different culture. Once a community has become established and begins to age, it must cope with the problems of an elderly population that may not be fully adapted to the country in which they live. At the same time, however, the community may also have considerable numbers of second-, third-, and subsequent-generation members who wish to remain associated with their ancestral community. Hence it must focus on the problems of aging, but it cannot afford to do so exclusively.

Indeed, a population such as the Chaldean community, which receives a continuing stream of new immigrants each year, includes all of these groups at once! The community must continue to deal with the problems of new immigrants and their children. In addition, however, the community now must assist its elderly members in coping with the problems of aging in a society whose ways of dealing with old age are dramatically different from those left behind in the country of origin, not to mention the problems of coping with the health issues of old age when many health care providers speak a different language. Hence the community must deal with the cultural identity needs of well-established members, the needs of new immigrants, and the problems of an aging community—all at the same time.

Problems of a Community with Continuing Migration

Since the change in American migration laws in 1968, Middle Eastern communities have come to resemble the Mexican and Puerto Rican communities, in that all of them continue to receive a constant influx of new members. This characteristic distinguishes these communities from older ethnic groups, such as the Irish, the Germans, the Italians, the Polish, and other immigrants who came to the United States in the later nineteenth and early twentieth centuries. Most such communities experienced a massive influx of new members for four or five decades, after which migration slowed or stopped. Such communities adopted patterns to assist new migrants during these early years. Later, as the number of migrants diminished, they accommodated their community institutions for use by second, third, or subsequent generations of members.

The Chaldean community, however, includes persons whose ancestors arrived in the United States nearly a century ago—as well as others who arrived only yesterday. Hence community institutions must adapt to serve both new immigrants and well-established members of the community. Furthermore, changes occur, both in the United States and in the country of origin. Residents in both places adapt to these differing conditions, such that the type of immigrant coming to the United States changes over time. Hence, the ethnic community must become aware of the differing characteristics of the new immigrants, as well as the new set of difficulties that they face.

Migration a century ago was a difficult process, and males were usually the first to come. In recent years, as travel has become easier and women more independent, women and families are more likely to migrate. Economic opportunities are also different now from those the earliest Chaldean migrants faced. These first migrants were primarily village people with few contacts outside the original town. Following the establishment of the nation of Iraq and the Second World War, however, there was considerable migration out of the original village, not only to the United States but also to the major urban centers of Iraq, particularly Baghdad, Mosul, and Basra. Former residents of these cities are a significant portion of today's Chaldean migrants to Detroit.

Hence, more recent Chaldean migrants have been urban Iraqi citizens, rather than residents of a rural area. Recent immigrants are more accustomed than the earlier immigrants to the complex, urban, industrial environment. They have had more contact than preceding immigrants with persons from other towns, and in particular, with Muslims, who constitute the dominant religious group in Iraq. These experiences in Iraqi cities have accustomed them to a complex, industrial economy with a diversity of groups, and prepared them better for the urban diversity and industrial economy of an urban center like Detroit. Many recent Chaldean immigrants are already well educated in a variety of professions.

The most obvious change in Chaldean immigrants to Detroit, however, is in the area of language. In Iraq, like other Arab Muslim nations, the official language is Arabic. Chaldean immigrants since the mid-twentieth century have been educated in the national schools of Iraq and speak Arabic. Many immigrants who have arrived since the 1960s do not even know the Chaldean (Aramaic) language. Indeed, some of the Chaldean churches have begun offering courses to introduce the Chaldean language, not only to American-born Chaldeans but also to recent immigrants who know only Arabic.

The reasons for Chaldean migration today are in some ways different from but in many ways the same as those that motivated their predecessors. Migration analysts have long pointed to the fact that immigration is motivated both from within and from without. This has been called the "push-pull" theory.[43] That is, migrants are motivated, in part, by the unpleasant conditions in which they live in the country of origin. Persons who are generally well situated at home are unlikely to migrate. It is those who are dissatisfied with the status quo who are likely to leave. This is the "push" factor. On the other hand, they are also motivated by the belief that things will be better elsewhere—the "pull factor."

The earliest Chaldean immigrants came to the United States in a quest for better economic conditions and to escape what they perceived to be a tense environment for Christians in a predominantly Muslim world. Like others in the late nineteenth and early twentieth centuries, they had heard that America was the land of opportunity—a solution to the difficulties they faced at home. As one early Chaldean immigrant told me, "Over there, they think the streets here are paved with gold. So they think, why don't you sweep half a block for me!"

Conditions in Iraq a century later are markedly different. Reportedly there has been more acceptance of religious diversity, and the economy is no longer agrarian. However, as the French say, *"plus ca change, le plus le meme chose"* (the more things change, the more they stay the same). In the closing decades of the twentieth century, Iraq became a war-torn country. Iraq's wars with Iran and the Kurds; continued tensions between the Arab states and Israel; the Gulf War with the United States; continued concerns with United Nations weapon surveillance; and the second war between Iraq and the United States all made Iraq a tense environment, and provided a constant pressure to leave. The Kurdish conflict was particularly difficult for the Detroit community, because Telkaif is located in the Kurdish area. Iraq, and the Arab world in general, were even more troubled than they had been a century earlier.

Whatever Americans' feelings about Iraq's leaders, there is no doubt that its people have been suffering. Supplies of food and medicine have been in short supply for more than a decade, and many families have lost sons and brothers to these wars. United Nations' estimates suggest that about 1.5 million people died in Iraq between 1990 and 1998, and two to three times that number remain at risk.[44] Indeed, Chaldean community representatives have expended considerable amounts of money and effort to provide humanitarian assistance to relatives and friends back in Iraq. Not trusting either Iraqi or international programs to carry out this aid, they have sponsored several trips to take the supplies directly to people they know in Telkaif, Mosul, and other areas.

As we move into the first decade of the twenty-first century, matters have gone from bad to worse. The second Iraq War is worse than the first, and one cannot pick up a newspaper or turn on the television without learning of new, more serious developments there. Consequently, there is even more impetus for Chaldeans to leave Iraq. The "pull factor" is also operating. Friends and relatives already in Detroit beckon to those remaining in Iraq to join the U.S. community. Some Chaldeans assert proudly, "All our family is here now!" Numerous Chaldean families look forward to the day when they can make the same claim. It is not inaccurate to state that many Chaldeans long for the day when they can say that they have recreated the Chaldean community on U.S. soil.[45]

In the meantime, the Chaldean community also receives a constant stream of information about their country of origin. Among the early-twentieth-century immigrant groups, which lost contact rather quickly with their countries of origin, knowledge of the homeland soon turned to mythology, often with little basis in reality. With a constant influx of new immigrants, however, the Chaldean community is in constant contact with the culture of its country of origin. Middle Eastern communities have a constant stream of new arrivals providing up-to-date information about the country of origin. For the Chaldeans, this means they are continually receiving information about the changes that have occurred in Iraq over the years, including disturbing reports about conditions there. This only increases their resolve to bring the remainder of their families to the United States. The influx of recent Chaldean immigrants also means that the community now has a greater number of members who speak Arabic rather than Chaldean.

Impact of Immigration Laws

Any immigrant community in the United States is dramatically influenced by immigration laws. In the past, Middle Eastern immigrants have been greatly disadvantaged by these laws. Such groups began their communal trek to the United States at approximately the same time that restrictions were being placed on immigration. The so-called quota system was introduced in 1923, limiting immigration.[46] These limits were based on the number of persons already in the United States from that nation of origin. Areas such as the Middle East that had few residents here received only a nominal quota of one hundred per year. Consequently, these were lean years for Chaldean immigration. Immigration in general was also limited by the Second World War.

The student visas allowed following the Second World War brought about an increase in Chaldean immigration, as persons from Iraq, usually males, came to the United States on student visas, married members of the Detroit community, and changed their status to permanent immigrant. However, the greatest assistance to Chaldean immigration has been the 1965 immigration law, which removed the national origin quotas. This law limited only the overall number of immigrants allowed into the United States, rather than limiting the number from any given nation.

Like the quota system, the 1965 law gave preference to prospective immigrants with special occupational skills or relatives already living in the United States. Obviously, the extensive family contacts of Chaldean immigrants continue to put them at considerable advantage under these provisions. The new laws also made provisions for refugee permits for persons fleeing religious or political persecution.[47] As with any type of migration (even within a single nation), aspiring migrants with contacts at the destination point have a great advantage. They are aware of changes in conditions (including legal requirements), and have contacts there who can help them with the process. Consequently, both the increased numbers allowed to enter and the refugee permits have been boons to the Chaldean community.

The Impact of Community Size and Diversity

The enormous increase in its size, in and of itself, has had a considerable impact on the Chaldean community. While there may be debates over the accuracy of Chaldean population statistics, there is no question that the community is radically different today than it was fifty years ago. Half a century ago, everyone in the community knew everyone else. Now this is impossible. At that time, new arrivals could be fairly certain that the community would be able to place them in a job. Today their sheer numbers make that impossible as well. The community has faced the need to establish formal institutions to deal with problems formerly handled on an informal basis. There are now formal classes in the English language and social programs to help immigrants adjust to American society and culture and find employment.

The Arabic language that new immigrants bring with them prompts another set of difficulties, as community members argue which is the appropriate ethnic language. These differences between early and recent immigrants have generated a great deal of dissension within the community. With its growth in size, the Chaldean community has also become more visible to the Metropolitan Detroit community as a whole. In the early 1960s, prior to the change in immigration laws and the major influx of Chaldeans, most Detroiters had never even heard of the Chaldeans. Today the community is much more visible, and sometimes this has brought about negative reactions on the part of outsiders.

There are also positive aspects to this phenomenal community growth. With a larger population, the community can afford to provide more opportunities to introduce its culture and language to its members, including those born here. In effect, the community is forced to maintain a set of institutions to provide the newcomers with all of the services that ethnic communities have always provided to new arrivals.

The need to provide such services has led to a considerable growth in community institutions. This can best been seen through the growth in the Chaldean Church, from a single Chaldean church in the 1940s, to a full Chaldean diocese with a bishop and six parishes to serve the community. Social organizations include the Chaldean-Iraqi Association of Michigan, the Chaldean American Ladies of Charity, the Chaldean/American Youth Club, and the Chaldean Knights of Columbus, to mention a few—so many that there is now a Chaldean Federation to attempt to unite them. The Chaldean-Iraqi Association operates a social club and hall (Southfield Manor) and a golf club (Shenandoah Country Club). The Chaldean Ladies of Charity was instrumental in founding a Chaldean home for the elderly located on the grounds of Mother of God Church, and has also developed family service programs, providing information on drug and substance abuse and family violence to families.[48] The Arab-American and Chaldean Council and the Chaldean Federation both offer a variety of social services. Several periodicals now provide information to the Chaldean community. They include the *Chaldean News* (in English) and the *Detroit Middle East Newspaper* (in Arabic). Mid-East media also broadcasts programs in Arabic. Arabic-speaking Chaldeans also have access to other Arabic publications serving the large Middle East population in the Detroit area, such as the *Arab-American News,* published in Dearborn, Michigan, and on the CNN Internet site *http://arabic .cnn.com.* Chaldeans can also find news specific to Chaldean and Assyrian Christians at *http:www.aina.org* (Assyrian International News Agency) and *http:www.assyrianchristians.com.* These institutions serve not only to assist new arrivals but also to unite the community as a whole. The constant influx of new members is a continual reminder of what it means to be Chaldean, prompting even American-born Chaldeans to be aware of their heritage.

Coping with an Aging Community

While it deals with the problems of its new arrivals, the Chaldean community cannot ignore its older members. Immigration in the early twentieth century was difficult, so most immigrants were young, having left their aging parents behind. Consequently, in the early years of an immigrant community, youth predominates. As the early arrivals aged, they were largely cared for by their own families. However, Chaldeans, like the U.S. population as a whole, have benefited from the increasing life expectancy. Hence an increasingly large portion of the Chaldean population is of retirement age, and many are experiencing the health and social difficulties of old age. In 1990, the Michigan Department of Services to the Aging commissioned a study of Arabic-speaking elderly in the Detroit area, including the Chaldeans.[49] This study provides some insight into the patterns of aging in a relatively new ethnic community such as that of the Chaldeans.

In many ways, Chaldean elderly were similar to the elderly in the American population as a whole. They were relatively healthy, but frequently had the chronic diseases of old age, which are difficult to treat. They rarely allowed these health problems to interfere with their lives, although some reported needing help to carry out their daily activities. They also had a positive mental outlook, and did not feel that their health problems affected their lives. In general, growing old in the Chaldean community was a positive experience.

The daily activities of the elderly Chaldeans and the manner in which they received any needed assistance is an example of the general way of life in Chaldean families. While gerontologists have generally been aware of the family role in the care of the elderly, this factor is particularly obvious in ethnic communities, where the isolated elderly person is rarely found.[50] The Chaldean family is a good example of this.

Chaldean elders who needed assistance most commonly indicated that it was provided by a family member, usually a child or a spouse. In this community, one turns to an outsider (a friend or paid assistant) only in rare instances. It was also rare for Chaldean elders to turn to social agencies of any kind for assistance. Other than medical personnel, Chaldeans were not even aware of the existence of professional agency services. When they did discuss community services, they were more likely to prefer those that were provided within the context of the Chaldean community or church. This was not totally a language issue; that is, non-use of outside services was not due simply to the fact that agency personnel did not speak the Arabic or Chaldean language. Elderly Chaldeans were not comfortable with services that were offered in the Arabic language, either, because they generally saw these agencies as serving the Muslim community, with which most do not identify.

It was also obvious that Chaldean elders' participation in family life was not a one-way proposition. The Chaldean family system is a mutual process. Not only were Chaldean elders receiving assistance from other family members, but in many instances they were also providing it. Some were providing assistance to other elderly Chaldeans who, because of illness or disability, were more dependent than themselves. Most frequently the recipient of this assistance was a spouse. It could also be a parent or sibling, however, and some elderly Chaldeans were providing assistance to more than one other person.

Another aspect of Chaldean family life is its gender-specific character. Following the patterns found in other ethnic communities, Chaldean family patterns are largely delineated along gender lines. Thus it is often found that both males and females provide assistance to others in the family, but females almost always provide the assistance with cooking, housework, or personal care, while males provide money management and other financial assistance.[51]

Perhaps the most important finding from this study of elderly Chaldeans was its confirmation of the Chaldean community as a family- and religion-centered community. Nearly all reported going out at least weekly, usually to visit relatives. They also spent a great deal of time socializing on the telephone. On the other hand, few spoke about socializing with "friends" or "neighbors"—unless the neighbors happened also to be relatives. Those who did not live in Chaldean neighborhoods were more likely to go some distance to visit with relatives, rather than associate with unrelated neighbors. In general, most of these elders were definitely not socially isolated—indeed, they probably lacked sufficient time for all of their social activities!

There was a minority of Chaldean elders, however (approximately 20 to 30 percent, depending on the variable), who scored negatively on a variety of socio-emotional dimensions: they were more likely to be depressed or unhappy, to be disinterested in life, or to describe their mental health as poor. Interviewers also rated about 20 percent of the Chaldean elders as being mentally disoriented or in need of mental health care. In a group with so high a degree of social cohesiveness as the Chaldean community, the pain of these emotionally isolated individuals must be all the more severe.

This illustrates the difficulties of a community that depends exclusively on the family for assistance. When this family assistance is unavailable or ineffective, the problems become even more severe and insoluble. This is particularly true of family-generated problems, such as child-rearing problems or family violence. Chaldean community organizations need to focus their attention on identifying and serving the needs of this small but important segment of their elderly population who appear not to be well served by the close-knit Chaldean family structure. The senior housing opportunities and other services recently developed by the Chaldean Ladies of Charity and other agencies represent an important effort to deal with these problems.

Serving the Needs of a Larger, More Diverse Community

As it enters its second century, Detroit's Chaldean community faces the daunting task of serving a very different population from the one that it once served. Once an obscure little group of Middle Eastern immigrants, scarcely recognized by outsiders, they are now more widely recognized and are taken seriously as an important ethnic component in the Detroit Metropolitan Area. Not only is the community larger, it is also more diverse. There is a constant stream of new immigrants who need assistance in finding housing, jobs, and a means of adjusting to American society. As in American society as a whole, there are far more elderly members, with all of the needs they present. Of course, at the same time, they will want to retain the allegiance of second- and subsequent-generation Chaldeans to their ancestral heritage. Balancing the needs of these groups will require considerable effort and skill on the part of community leaders.

Redefining Community

This book began with an attempt to answer the following questions: Who are the Chaldeans? Where did they come from? And what relation do the ancient Chaldeans and Babylonians have with Detroit, Michigan, in the twenty-first century? The responses to these questions have provided a brief historical look at the ancestral claims of Detroit's Chaldean community. However, individual and group identity are not static characteristics. As social psychologists view it, they are the result of a social process that involves an interchange between individuals and their social contacts. People define who they are in response to the reactions others have to them.

A child establishes a sense of who he or she is through interacting with parents, siblings, grandparents, friends, and other members of the community. It is through their responses that the child comes to know what kind of person he or she is—that is, develops a sense of personal identity. Children learn that they are members of a particular family and belong to a specific racial, ethnic, or religious group; they also learn whether these characteristics are valued (or not valued) by others. If the child is a girl, she may come to believe that, because she is a girl, she should not be competitive or good in sports or math, or that she is expected to put the wishes of other people before her own. If the child is a boy, he may learn that he should be good in sports but not sensitive to the needs of others. Such messages are endless, and result in each of us having a sense of identity—who we are, what is expected of us, and where we fit into society as a whole.

For members of ethnic groups, the sense of *personal* identity— "Who *I* am"—is closely related to the sense of *group* identity—"Who *we* are." As one member of an ethnic group once put it: "I wondered who are all these people [her relatives and friends] were and how we fit together." While there has been some debate as to whether ethnic origins are still important in American society today, there appears to be considerable evidence that, at least for some, ethnic origin remains an important component of "who we are"—even to the point that the U.S. Census Bureau has had to change its manner of questioning about ethnic origins. Individuals' definitions about their ethnic identity are greatly influenced by the views of others about their racial and ethnic origins. Similarly, if the view of others about a specific ethnic origin should change in some manner, this is also likely to bring about a change in each individual's view of him- or herself.

While this may appear, at the outset, to be a simple process, it is actually very complicated. It may seem relatively simple for members of a group to determine who is or is not one of them, but there are often competing factors that come to bear on the issue. To be "Polish," for example, it may seem obvious that one must be born in Poland or in the United States of Polish parents. Yet what if only one parent was Polish? What of adopted children? Are there other characteristics that are critical? For example, most members of the American Polish community are Roman Catholic; Jews of Polish ancestry are not generally considered part of the Polish community. Similarly, Irish Catholics and Protestants are not usually grouped together.

Furthermore, ethnic identities are forged not only by patterns brought from the country of origin, but also by events that occur in the migration destination. Neither Germany nor Italy, for example, were unified nations when much of the German and Italian migration to the United States occurred. These immigrants came to the United States defining themselves as "Bavarians," or "Prussians," or "Sicilians," or "Milanese." Only after coming to the United States and finding that other Americans saw them as "Germans" or "Italians" did they begin to think of themselves in this manner. Hence, factors in both the country of origin and in the United States must be considered in order to understand the formation of the ethnic sense of identity.

Thus, an important point of our discussion concerns the manner in which the sense of identity of Chaldeans in the Detroit area has changed over time, in response to changes both within the Chaldean community and in the minds of American society as a whole. Chaldean ethnic identity cannot be discussed without controversy, and the major source of controversy is the conflict between their religious preference and their origin in an Arabic-speaking region.

Chaldeans are Arabs . . . Aren't They?

Most ethnic Americans base their identity on the geographic area of the world from which they originated. Since Chaldeans trace their origins to the Arabic-speaking Middle East, most Americans assume that Chaldeans must be Arabs. Within the Chaldean community, however, the sense of "who we are" is quite different. Indeed, most members of the community prefer to be called "Chaldeans," and resist use of the term "Arab" to identify themselves. The issue is not totally clear-cut, however, and considerable controversy has raged in the community at various times concerning their preferred method of identification.

Chaldean, Arab, Iraqi, and Telkeffee (denoting the original village of Telkaif) have all been used as identifying names by some members of the Chaldean community at one time or another. Discussions about the proper term of identification may become quite heated, even generating splits between friends or family members. More recent immigrants tend to have a different sense of identity than do the earliest arrivals. The preferred term also tends to vary over time, depending upon the current state of international affairs and conditions in the Middle East. The high degree of flux and unrest in the region as a whole is a major factor in the controversy. At least three factors serve as major points of identity for residents of Middle Eastern nations: village of origin, nation of origin, and the pan-Arab movement. These will serve as a convenient starting point for our analysis of Chaldean identity patterns.[52]

For generations, lasting until the early years of the twentieth century, residents of the Middle East defined themselves in terms of their village or regional origins. Communication between persons from different villages and regions was rare, and people viewed themselves and their world in local terms. There was little social interchange, and often considerable antagonism, between some of these towns. In fact, social interchange was complicated by the fact that residents of many of these regions spoke different dialects, or even different languages. Hence, Telkeffes spoke a dialect of Aramaic, while the dominant language of the Middle East was Arabic. Furthermore, the current nations of the Middle East did not exist until the arrival of the European colonial powers in the late nineteenth and early twentieth centuries.

Hence, the first Chaldeans to come to Detroit, who arrived before 1930, saw themselves as residents of the village of Telkaif. They intermarried with other villagers and rarely developed ties outside the town. They had no sense of a wider world. Iraq, as a nation, did not exist. Thus the initial identifying term for community members was "Telkeffee," the term often used by the earliest immigrants to the United States. During the early and middle years of the twentieth century, their influence in the Detroit community was strong, and the sense of being from the village of Telkaif was a major focus of identity for Detroit's Chaldeans.

Times change, however, and the Middle East was becoming increasingly urban and industrial. Its residents were also becoming more aware of persons from other towns and regions, and many were living outside of the original village, in major Iraqi cities, such as Baghdad, Mosul, and Basra. They were being educated in the national schools of Iraq, where they learned the Arabic language. Immigrants in this period, who began migrating to the United States after the end of the Second World War, were less likely to think of themselves in local or regional terms. They spoke Arabic, and many did not even know the village language. In fact, some have been heard to comment, "Who wants to be a Telkeffee? It's just a crumby little town!" They grew up in Iraq during its major period of growth as a separate nation. They thought of themselves in the broader terms of national origin, in which people from a broad spectrum of regions participate. The influence of

American society also played a role. "Telkeffee" meant nothing to most Americans with whom community members had contact. Iraq, on the other hand, was a recognizable nation. Other Americans were of German or English or Irish origin. Hence many Chaldeans came to think of themselves as "Iraqis." Identification of themselves as Iraqis is generally more palatable to Chaldeans than is identification as Arabs, although the continued conflict between the United States and Iraq has altered this pattern somewhat.

Concurrent with the development of the Middle Eastern nations, however, was the development throughout the entire Middle East of a sense of common origin among all persons from an Arabic-speaking background, whatever their specific national origin. In a very real sense, these two themes are in conflict with each other, because the national view calls for unity among members of a specific nation (Iraq, or Lebanon, or Jordan, for example), while pan-Arabism calls for Arabs from all of these nations to unite and work together as a single unit. This movement intensified as the various Arab states dealt with the presence of the State of Israel, and encouraged Chaldeans to identify themselves as Arabs, rather than as either Telkeffees or Iraqis.

The notion of pan-Arabism raises another issue in the development of Chaldean community identity, however. The reader will note that I still have not mentioned the term most often used: Chaldean. While the early immigrants tended to call themselves "Telkeffees," and some later immigrants preferred the term "Iraqi," to denote a national identity, few Chaldeans have chosen to identify themselves as Arabs. This factor has placed them at odds with large segments of the Middle Eastern communities in the United States.

Chaldean reluctance to identify themselves as Arabs raises another issue about patterns of ethnic identification. As noted previously, national or pan-Arab movements require that individuals alter their sense of "who we are" to include persons with whom they have not had a long history of association. Tribal groups who have long mistrusted persons from nearby groups or villages often find it difficult to give up these old antagonisms. They are unlikely to do so unless there is a compelling reason. In the past, some groups have joined together with former local enemies in order to impede the expansion of colonial powers in their regions. The greater the difference between groups, however, the more difficult such new alliances are likely to be.

Chaldeans have several reasons for not identifying themselves as Iraqis or Arabs. Among these could be listed geography, language, and religion. In terms of geography, the province of Mosul, in which Telkaif is located, has not been closely identified with the nation of Iraq since its foundation. The province is characterized by considerable variation in language and culture. There are other towns in the area like Telkaif that are predominately Christian and Aramaic-speaking, rather than Muslim and Arabic-speaking. This area is also home to the Kurds, who have had a long-standing dispute with the Iraqi government, including all out war at times. Hence Chaldeans are predisposed by geography and language to reject both the Iraqi and the Arabic identity.

With Chaldeans, the religious factor makes it particularly difficult for them to identify either with other Iraqis or with Arabs as a whole. For better or for worse, Arabic culture and the Arabic-speaking nations are associated, in the minds of most people, including the Chaldeans, with the Muslim religion. As Christians, Chaldeans have long felt a divergence between themselves and Muslims. Indeed, many early Chaldean immigrants spoke of experiencing harassment, or even persecution, at the hands of Muslim neighbors.

As previously indicated, the Catholic religion is an extremely important component of the Chaldean community. Most have found it very difficult to separate the Arabic language and culture from the Muslim religion. This has not been true of other Christian groups in the Arab world. Some Lebanese, Jordanian, and Egyptian Christians, for example, have found it quite comfortable to be identified as "Christian Arabs." Detroit's Chaldeans, for the most part, however, have not. A possible reason might be their numbers. If, for example, there are only a few thousand Jordanians in an area, divided between Muslims and Christians, it is probably easier to bring them together as a single group. Because of their large numbers in the Detroit area, however, Chaldeans have no need to expand their notion of community.

There was a period in the 1970s and early 1980s during which some members of the Detroit Chaldean community began to define themselves as Christian Arabs. During this period there was a high rate of immigration. (The community nearly tripled in size from 1967 to 1978.) Most of these new immigrants had been born and reared in Iraqi cities, where they had learned the Arabic language and culture. Although they practiced the Chaldean religion, most did not speak or understand the Chaldean language. Some rejected the Chaldean culture, pointing out that the Chaldean language was only a regional language, and everyone would have to speak Arabic if they visited Iraq. Identifying as Arabs was an option for these new immigrants, but this often placed them at odds with relatives who had been in Detroit for some time.

Being an Iraqi or Arab at the Turn of the Millennium

By the 1990s, however, open identification either as Arabs or as Iraqis had declined considerably in the Chaldean community. One of the major reasons was the outbreak of the Gulf War in 1991. Chaldeans were placed in the uncomfortable position of dealing with hostilities between their old homeland and their new. Being identified as Iraqi was less likely to be seen as a viable option. This continued throughout the 1990s, and has increased in intensity as new hostilities have developed in the first decade of the twenty-first century. Many second- and third-generation Chaldeans, who never thought of themselves as either Iraqis or as Arabs, have been asked to explain their background. Some have had to consult their parents and grandparents in order to understand the conflicting identities.

Considering the average American's lack of knowledge about the Middle East, there tends to be little differentiation in their minds between Arabs, Chaldeans, Iraqis, and immigrants from any of the other nations in the region. Americans see Iraq and the Arabs as the enemy, and Chaldeans are associated with them. Formation of ethnic identity patterns in the United States is influenced at least as much by the people one encounters in this country as by historical, geographical, religious, or linguistic patterns remembered from the old country. If their American neighbors consistently identify Chaldeans as Arabs or Iraqis, sooner or later, many Chaldeans are likely to accept the designation. On the other hand, if these designations are negative and lead to their being viewed as "the enemy," the identity will very likely be resisted if at all possible.

As previously mentioned, however, in the minds of most Americans, Chaldeans are likely to be recognized as Arabs and Iraqis— whether they like it or not. In fact, most Americans do not distinguish among the many different subgroups of the Arabic-speaking population. Arabs may differentiate by religious preference or national origin, but to most Americans, they are all lumped together, and all the terms suggest the same cluster of characteristics: Middle Eastern, Arabic-speaking, and Muslim. That they have different national origins, languages and religions is rarely recognized.

This is largely the situation in which the Chaldean community finds itself at the dawn of the new millennium. Like the Japanese-Americans during World War II, they are the local representatives of a hated foreign country with which the United States is at war. This presents problems both here and in Iraq. During the 1991 Gulf War, many Chaldean families were placed in the uncomfortable dilemma of having relatives fighting on both sides of the Gulf War. They have heard stories of the impact that American embargoes have had on their relatives left in Iraq. Many Chaldeans came to the United States as refugees during the 1990s, bringing more stories of the suffering left behind. This is likely to leave the Chaldeans even more anxious to differentiate themselves from Iraq and the Arab movement, as well as to move as many of their relatives as possible to their newly created Chaldean homeland in Metropolitan Detroit.

Chaldeans also fear for their own safety at home. During the Gulf War, homes and stores belonging to Chaldeans (and other Arab-Americans as well) were reportedly looted or fire-bombed. Government officials contacted community members and others familiar with the Iraqi community to obtain information about possible community involvement in Iraqi spying activities. Rumors circulated that Americans of Iraqi descent would be relocated and their property confiscated, similar to the treatment of Japanese during World War II. The rumors even stated that Louisiana had already been chosen as the relocation site.[53] A well-known business, Melody Dairy, owned by

Chaldean Michael George, was the target of an extensive federal investigation; when the investigation ended with only minor violations being found, many analysts, both in the Arab and Chaldean communities and in the business community at large, expressed the opinion that the investigation had been politically motivated.[54]

While a major disruption of their lives did not occur, the threat of such a disruption left community members uneasy. Chaldeans remain divided about the 2003 Iraq War. Many support the war, since Saddam Hussein was not widely loved. However, they continue to fear the consequences of conflict between their new homeland and their country of origin, including possible reprisals against the community here, as well as the risk of renewed turmoil for family members left behind. Many Chaldeans have relatives who have been killed or injured as a result of the two wars with the United States.[55] The United Nations estimates that half a million children under five years of age have died as a result of the sanctions imposed by the U.S. government.[56]

As violence in Iraq continues, Chaldeans remain apprehensive about their homeland, particularly about family members there. Government officials both in Iraq and the United States assure the community that their homeland is being rebuilt, that conditions are improving under the interim government, and, in particular, that ethnic minorities, such as Chaldeans and Assyrians, will be protected under the new constitution.[57] Chaldean and Muslim religious leaders insist that they are united in their commitment to freedom of religion for the Christian minority in Iraq.[58]

However, violence in Iraq continues. Members of the Iraqi Governing Council have been assassinated.[59] And the promises of ethnic minority protection appear empty in the light of bombing of Chaldean and other Christian churches; businesses run by Christians, especially liquor, fashion, and music stores which violate Muslim traditions; and the harassment of Christian women who do not observe the Muslim tradition of wearing headscarves.[60] Chaldean leaders in the Detroit area have met with U.S. leaders, such as Senator Carl Levin, to request assistance for the protection of their people in Iraq.[61] Even the new Iraqi flag is troublesome. It bears a symbolic representation of the Islamic majority and the Kurdish minority, but in spite of the constitutional commitment to ethnic equality, there is no symbolic representation of Iraq's Chaldeans and Assyrians.[62] Hence some Chaldeans wonder what the promise of a democratic government in Iraq holds for their people.

Iraqi immigrants to Western nations are often suggested as a valuable source of assistance in the rebuilding of Iraq. Undoubtedly some Iraqi-Chaldeans would be interested in such roles, but most seem more interested in continuing to build their lives in the United States. The war seems more likely to produce increased assistance to relatives in Iraq, including efforts to transplant even more Chaldeans to the Detroit area.

Contributions of the Chaldean Community to Detroit and Michigan

What is the legacy of nearly a century of Chaldean immigration to Metropolitan Detroit and Michigan? What have Chaldeans and Chaldean culture given to the area? Conversely, have there been drawbacks to their involvement in Detroit and Michigan? Contributions could be mentioned in the areas of citizenship, business, and general culture, and overall the contributions appear to far outweigh the drawbacks.

Chaldean Contributions as Citizens

What America has a right to expect from immigrants is basically what every community has a right to expect from all of its residents: that they become good citizens, work for a living, obey the laws, pay their taxes, and raise their children to do the same when they grow up. In this regard, Chaldeans have a general reputation as law-abiding citizens who run their businesses, take care of their families, and do not create trouble for the community. They have also contributed to the advancement of their communities through sending numerous members to institutions of higher education and into advanced professions. Many Chaldeans have also served in the military in their newly chosen homeland—including during the Gulf War and the U.S.-Iraq War, when many feared they would find themselves facing relatives and friends over the butt of a rifle.

Chaldean Economic Contributions to Detroit and Michigan

Perhaps the most obvious benefit that the Chaldeans have brought to the area is related to the business environment. *Crain's Detroit Business* notes that the Detroit area has about 275,000 Arab-Americans, 15,000 of whom own businesses, and 60 percent of whom are in executive, managerial, or similar positions. Consequently, the Chaldean community is increasingly being recognized as a major untapped market by financial institutions.[63] The *2000–2001 Chaldean Directory* lists 466 grocery store owners, 456 owners of other types of businesses, 31 physicians, 33 attorneys, and 86 other professionals (dentists, teachers, pharmacists, and so on). Chaldeans have also begun to move into the political realm with the election of Richard Sulaka as a City Council member for the city of Warren, and Diane Dickow D'Agostini as a District Judge in Oakland County.[64]

Chaldean stores represent a considerable proportion of Arab-American businesses. Today's stores are located both in the city of Detroit and in suburban areas from Ecorse to Pontiac to Port Huron. It is difficult to estimate the economic contribution Chaldeans make each year to the Detroit and Michigan economy through the food distribution industry. One store owner estimated that his 30,000-square-foot store grossed $7–8 million dollars worth of revenue per year.[65] Even if one assumes this to be one of the larger operations, the 466 store owners listed in the *2000–2001 Chaldean Directory* obviously make a substantial contribution each year to the Southeast Michigan economy.

In effect, Chaldean grocery stores have been the mainstay of food services for the city of Detroit for the better part of the last half of the twentieth century. In the 1960s and 1970s the large grocery chains largely abandoned the city of Detroit.[66] In part, this was a result of the 1967 Detroit riot. However, it was also related to the fact that the chains preferred to develop extremely large stores, and the amount of land needed for such facilities was not available in the already developed central city. For the Chaldeans, the facilities left by the departing chain stores offered an excellent opportunity to expand. Many of the large Chaldean stores developed during this period.

Whatever the reason, for a large part of the later twentieth century, there were few grocery chain stores in Detroit. A few were developed in the 1990s.[67] For the better part of this period, however, there would have been no food service in Detroit, but for the Chaldean stores. There were often complaints from customers that such independent stores were not the most effective food service providers. Yet without them there would have been no food service in Detroit at all, and this was a community in which large portions of the population were lacking in efficient means of transportation that would have allowed them to commute to the suburban areas where the chains preferred to locate.

Chaldeans could also be a model for the development of economically independent ethnic communities. They have developed enormously effective mechanisms for introducing new members to economic enterprises and helping them to get established. They have done this not primarily by supporting the newcomers and providing jobs in existing enterprises but by helping them become established in their own independent enterprises.[68] The vast majority of Chaldean businesses are independent or family-held. Contrary to the beliefs of many Detroiters, Chaldean grocery businesses are nearly all independently owned and operated. Chaldean food stores are not the Chaldean equivalent of Kroger or Farmer Jack, although some have become associated with smaller chains such as "Spartan Stores."[69]

Hence the Chaldean community largely provided assistance that helped its members develop into independent business operators. They have provided this assistance in numerous ways, as Salman Sesi indicated in an interview with *Crain's Detroit Business*,[70] including locating financial resources, developing community-based loans, identifying appropriate locations for grocery stores, and helping establish contacts with suppliers of grocery items and other supplies, such as refrigeration equipment, linen supplies, and so on. Opening an independent business is a complicated operation, and assistance from knowledgeable community members can mean the difference between spectacular success and utter failure. The Chaldean community could well be a model for community economic development, not only for ethnic communities but for small cities and neighborhoods as well.

Chaldeans also provide a good example for developing new enterprises from the original ones. Community economic enterprises are no longer limited to grocery stores. Chaldeans were among the forerunners in expanding into new food store operations, such as party stores, convenience stores, combination pharmacy and grocery store operations, and gas station/food store combinations. Some community members also developed extensive business enterprises that specialize in supplying the grocery business in some of the areas mentioned previously, such as providing business realty consultation, accounting services, wholesale groceries, and other supplies needed in the stores. For example, Central Alarm Signal, Inc., which provides burglary alarm service, is a Chaldean enterprise that began as a service to store owners. Melody Farms, Inc., a well-known Chaldean enterprise located in Livonia, Michigan, posted revenues of $144.7 million in 1996.[71] The Jonna Companies, devoted to real estate development and construction, were recently selected to carry out major development of a sixty-five-acre site in Novi for Providence Hospital.[72] Chaldean economic enterprises illustrate an amazing ability and willingness to take advantage of economic expansion opportunities.

Blacks and Chaldean Conflicts in Grocery Store Areas

There has been considerable resentment, at times, against Chaldeans for their food service in Detroit. Much of this resentment stems from the nature of the *independent* food service business. Customers examine the groceries available in an independent food store and the prices charged. They then compare them with the wider array of goods, coupled with the more reasonable prices generally charged in large supermarket chains such as Kroger, Farmer Jack, and Meijer, all food chains located in the Detroit area. Independent stores are found wanting in both range of selection and price level.

Chaldean store owners have often been criticized for this difference. African Americans who live in the areas served by the stores claim that Chaldeans (or "Syrians" or "Arabs," as they are sometimes called)

are cheating their customers. While it is possible that some store owners are, in fact, cheating customers, these problems are, to a great
extent, inherent in the nature of the independent, as opposed to the
chain store operation. With their enormous buying power—indeed,
with their own food processing resources—the grocery chains can offer
a much wider array of choices and much more economical prices than
any independent store, no matter how efficient. Hence Chaldeans are
often blamed for a situation that is beyond their control.

All the same, however, there have been unfortunate confrontations
between Chaldean store owners and their largely African-American
customers. These have included Chaldean store owners and employees
killed by black customers, as well as the reverse. Chaldean store owners also suffered a number of losses during the Detroit riot in 1967.
Chaldean store owners and their neighbors have attempted to deal
with these problems through a number of mechanisms. Some of these
have included involvement in neighborhood community organizations; charitable assistance, such as providing holiday food baskets for
the poor in local areas; and attempting to hire local people to work in
the stores. Reports of negative incidents appear to have decreased during the late 1990s.[73]

Culture-Related Controversies between Chaldeans and Other Suburbanites

Whenever persons of different cultural backgrounds come into contact
with each other there is opportunity for conflict or disagreement. These
conflicts often arise from differences in the cultures of the different
groups. Two aspects of Chaldean culture have occasionally brought
them into conflict with other groups in the Detroit area.

Chaldean culture, and Middle Eastern culture in general, tends to
be rather "loud." Chaldean families have many family gatherings,
largely centered in the home. Because store owners work late, these
noisy parties often last long into the night. For many of their neighbors,
this can mean that Chaldeans are very annoying neighbors. When I first
studied the Chaldean community in the 1960s and 1970s, many of them
lived in Detroit neighborhoods, and I heard these complaints from

their primarily African-American neighbors. In the past quarter century, Chaldeans have moved to suburban areas, and their new neighbors, both whites and African Americans, continue to have the same complaints: that Chaldean families are large and that they have many loud parties, with many relatives and friends visiting at all hours of the night.

A more critical point of contention for Chaldeans and their suburban neighbors has centered around Chaldean views of education. Chaldeans who have moved into suburban communities tend to be quite successful business people and they are able to live in the more affluent areas. Most Chaldeans have moved into communities in Oakland County: Oak Park, Southfield, Birmingham, Bloomfield Hills, Farmington Hills, and so on. Several of these areas were established by upper-middle-class professionals who reached their level of affluence largely by virtue of their education. To complicate matters further, many of these communities were heavily Jewish, with the particular commitment to education that characterizes the Jewish community.

In these communities, education was the key to socioeconomic advancement, not only for those who founded the communities but for their children as well. Consequently, these communities developed excellent school systems, with emphasis on college preparation, Advanced Placement courses, and special programs in science, music, and art. Residents developed these educational systems at great personal expense, voting for high property taxes to develop and maintain these outstanding schools.

The arrival of their Chaldean neighbors presented them with a surprise, however. Chaldeans had a very different view of advancement and education. Many of today's Chaldeans are professional people and value education highly. Yet the earlier Chaldeans were self-made businessmen with very little education, and they saw little need for it. Many felt that going into business was far preferable to going to college. They could provide numerous examples of their children's friends who were struggling to pay their way through college, while their own children, with no college education, were already well established in business, with their own homes, families, and expensive cars. What good was college? They wanted their children to take business math, not calculus.

Furthermore, schools that Chaldean children attended now had to pay attention to bilingual education, problems of truancy, and dropouts— issues that had never been a concern in the past.

From the 1960s through the 1980s, these variant views created considerable tension in some suburban school districts. Residents, teachers, administrators, and consultants for the schools all were concerned about the "Chaldean problem."[74] In the 1990s, however, as Chaldeans moved into a wider variety of occupations and professions, they came to resemble their suburban neighbors more closely, and these types of confrontations became less frequent.

Conclusion

Since the major institutions of the Chaldean community are family and church, it is important to point out that Chaldean commitment to home and family, as exemplified in Chaldean culture, could serve as a model for other communities. This fact was brought to my attention by the late Professor Elizabeth Hood, of the College of Education at Wayne State University, who invited me to make a presentation on the Chaldean community to her class on diversity in education. One student in the class asked, in an exceptionally crude manner, "What have Chaldeans ever done for this community [Detroit and Michigan]?" Somewhat taken aback, I mentioned their role in the grocery business. Dr. Hood, however, had a different, and, I believe, a much better answer. She went on to expand on how impressed she was with Chaldeans' commitment to family. Dr. Hood, an African American, commented that she had attended a number of Chaldean weddings with her husband, the late Nicholas Hood, a former member of the Detroit City Council. These experiences had shown her how devoted they were to family.

She then told a story from one of the weddings she had recently attended. "At the reception," she said, "the father of the bride stood up and announced that he had a gift to give to the groom: his own grocery

The groom and his family generally play a much greater role in Chaldean wedding celebrations than in most American weddings. While Chaldean weddings now follow American customs, some remnants remain of traditional Chaldean practice in which the groom's family paid for the wedding. Here Patrick Najor's friends participate in the Chaldean tradition of lifting the groom during his wedding reception. (Photo courtesy of Dr. Michelle Najor.)

store." Dr. Hood concluded by noting that, in her African-American community, "We would have waited a few years to see if the marriage lasted before we would have given such a gift. In the Chaldean community, however, this was not necessary, because Chaldean marriages last forever." Dr. Hood's message is an important one: The Chaldean people are an example of the importance of commitment to family values, and of religious traditions that support these values, especially today, when many have lost a sense of the important role of these institutions in our lives. The extensive contact between elderly Chaldeans and their families is another dimension of this important family tradition.

A Unique Social, Cultural, Economic, and Historical Heritage

Chaldean culture and social patterns have contributed a great deal to the richness of the Detroit Metropolitan area and Southeast Michigan.

These contributions cover many areas, from church and family to the economy. In addition, Chaldean origins in ancient Mesopotamia bring a historical dimension to their community that is not represented by other ethnic communities in the area. Chaldeans themselves, long focusing their attention primarily on the adjustment process to a new environment, are becoming more aware and appreciative of the unique contribution that their Chaldean heritage presents to Detroit and Michigan. As they near their centennial celebration as a community, the Iraqi-Chaldean Association of Michigan is undertaking efforts to establish a cultural center to celebrate this heritage. They have much to offer and to build on in the diverse areas of their rich cultural heritage.

Chaldean-Style Food and Sample Recipes

haldean-style food is similar to that of other Middle Eastern Cuisines, including Lebanese, Syrian, and Greek. Typical foods include shish-kebab (cubes of beef or lamb placed on a skewer with vegetables and grilled); humos (see following recipe); and tabbouli (*tapula* in Chaldean—a salad composed of chopped parsley, cracked wheat, onions, tomatoes, and spices). Kibbeh (a pie made with ground meat and wheat and baked or fried) is made by other Middle Eastern groups, but Chaldeans make kibbeh in small patties that are boiled rather than baked (see recipe following). Rice, rather than potatoes, is a staple of most Middle Eastern cuisines, including that of the Chaldeans, and meals are accompanied by large quantities of pita bread. Rice mixed with ground meat is also used as a stuffing for vegetables, as in the recipe following. Some Chaldean cooks also use this stuffing for the traditional American turkey. The most typical Middle Eastern stuffed vegetables are stuffed grape leaves, called *dolma* in Arabic and *yupprugh* in the original Chaldean language.

Recipes provided here are adapted from Julia Najor, *Babylonian Cuisine: Chaldean Cookbook from the Middle East,* 2d ed. (Detroit: National Books International, 1981). I express my appreciation to Mrs. Najor and to the Chaldean Ladies of Charity for permission to quote from the book.

Humos Bi Tehneh (Chick Pea Dip)

2 to 3 cups canned chick peas
½ cup tahini (rashi) (ground sesame seeds)
salt and red pepper to taste
2–3 cloves garlic, crushed
¾ cup lemon juice (or to taste)
2 Tbsp. olive oil

Boil chick peas until soft. Mash peas and push through sieve. Add tahini. Mix well. Sprinkle with salt and pepper, and add garlic. Add lemon juice a small amount at a time. Mix well. Pour into serving dish and smooth, and pour olive oil over it. Garnish with tomatoes, radishes, parsley, etc. Usually served with pita bread. *Makes 3 servings.*

Chaldean Kibbeh (Meat and Wheat Pies)

Kibbeh Dough

2 Tbsp. salt mixed with 1 tablespoon baking soda
2 lbs. lean hamburger
2 Tbsp. quick Cream of Wheat
½ cup water
3½ cups fine cracked wheat, rinsed and drained
2 cups cold water (or more, as needed)

Combine salt/soda mixture, hamburger, Cream of Wheat, and ½ cup water. Cover and leave overnight in refrigerator. In the morning, mix in cracked wheat and 2 cups of cold water. Knead or grind mixture twice. Add more water little by little, if needed, until mixture is soft and smooth. Cover with wax paper while using. *Makes 20–24 patties.*

Kibbeh Stuffing

6 onions, finely chopped
2 Tbsp. butter or margarine
3 tsp. salt
½ to 1 tsp. black pepper (or to taste)

2 tsp. allspice

3 lbs. medium coarse ground beef or lamb

Fry onions in 2 tablespoons butter in six-quart saucepan. Add salt, pepper, and allspice, and brown. While still hot, add to meat and mix well. Chill before using. If desired, add ½ cup almonds and ½ cup raisins, both browned. *Note:* For a simpler Kibbeh stuffing, Mrs. Najor suggests combining 2 pounds coarse ground beef and 1 package of dry onion soup mix.

Take ¼ cup Kibbeh dough at a time and flatten into circles or cup in the hand. Stuff with ¼ cup of Kibbeh stuffing. Close circle around stuffing and press into patties. Boil 2 quarts of water with 3 teaspoons salt. Add Stuffed Kibbeh, six at a time, and cook until they float (about 20–25 minutes). *Note:* These kibbeh patties freeze well.

Dolma/Yuppruch (Stuffed Grape Leaves)

The typical Middle Eastern stuffed vegetables are grape leaves, but a wide variety of other vegetables may also be used, including eggplant, cucumbers, green peppers, onions, tomatoes, potatoes, turnips, and zucchini. Seeds and centers should be removed in preparation for stuffing. Cabbage leaves may also be stuffed like grape leaves. Grape leaves can be obtained in most Middle Eastern food stores. Mrs. Najor recommends using small vegetables, and parboiling onions (5 min.) and cabbage (3 min.) before stuffing. Vegetables should be prepared before beginning the stuffing. *Serves 5 to 7.*

Dolma Vegetables

1 lb. frozen grape leaves or 1-lb. jar of grape leaves

Other small vegetables (eggplant, onions, green peppers, squash, etc.) as desired

Dolma Stuffing

½ head garlic, chopped fine

½ large onion, chopped fine

½ green pepper, chopped fine

½ small hot red pepper, chopped fine

½ cup margarine or butter

1¾ 6-oz. cans of tomato paste

¼ tsp. black pepper

1 Tbsp. ground allspice

2 tomatoes, chopped fine

½ cup chopped parsley

2½ cups converted parboiled long-grain rice, washed and drained

1¾ lbs. coarse ground roasting beef or lamb

3 Tbsp. salt

¾ cups lemon juice

2 Tbsp. spearmint leaves, fresh or dry

2 Tbsp. fresh dill, or 1 Tbsp. dry

2 small hot peppers

Brown garlic, onion, green pepper, and hot red pepper in ¼ cup margarine. Add tomato paste, black pepper, and allspice, and brown. Add tomatoes, ¼ cup margarine, and parsley. Let cool. Mix onion mixture well with rice, meat, salt, and lemon juice. Add spearmint and dill.

Have ready for cooking dolma:

2 to 3 pieces short ribs

¼ cup vinegar, 1½ cups water for boiling ribs and draining

1 cup plus 2 Tbsp. lemon juice

¾ stick butter or margarine

Filling and Cooking

Spread a layer of grape leaves on bottom of eight-quart saucepan. Put remaining small hot red pepper over grape leaves. Boil short ribs in vinegar and water and put ribs over grape leaves. Stuff the grape leaves and vegetables one at a time. *For stuffing grape leaves:* place small amount of stuffing on edge of grape leaf where the stem is. Fold both sides inward, then fold the stem inward too; roll in the shape of a pencil, and place in pan. Layer the stuffed grape leaves and other vegetables over the ribs. Add the lemon juice and ¾ stick butter to eight-quart saucepan. Cover with aluminum foil and lid. Bring to a boil and cook for 1 hour on low heat. If there is too much water, remove lid and foil and cook until water is evaporated. Close lid and simmer for 10 minutes. Turn over on platter to serve. Mrs. Najor notes that this recipe freezes well.

Vegetarian Dolma

Meatless Dolma may be made by omitting the short ribs during the cooking process, and substituting the following for the ground beef or lamb in the above Dolma recipe:

4 small cans of mushrooms, fried
6–8 potatoes, peeled and cut small
3 cups canned chick peas without juice
2 cups diced celery, Swiss chard, or carrots may also be added
Shrimp may also be added to the saucepan with the Dolma if
desired.

Sesame Seed Candy

½ cup dark corn syrup
1 cup Celan (date syrup) or pancake syrup
3½ cups untoasted sesame seeds
1 tsp. ground cardamom

In a small, heavy saucepan cook corn syrup and date or pancake syrup over medium heat while stirring until candy thermometer registers 245° (about 20–25 minutes). Toast sesame seeds in frying pan over medium heat, stirring often. Add sesame seeds and cardamom to syrup and blend well. Spread on greased pan evenly. Let it cool, about 10 minutes. Sprinkle sesame seeds on board. Make a ball of the mixture, roll out on the board with a rolling pin to about ¼-inch thickness. Cut into squares. *Makes 30 squares.*

Chaldean Organizations and Contacts

Space limitations prohibit a complete listing of all Chaldean organizations. This should be seen as only a sampling, and I apologize for any omissions. Organizations have been grouped into church-related and secular organizations. I have not listed private businesses owned by Chaldeans.

Churches and Church-Related Organizations

- Chaldean Diocese in the United States, Chancery Office, 25063 Berg Rd., Southfield, MI 48034; (248) 351-0440; *http://www.chaldeandiocese.org*
- Chaldean Knights of Columbus—St. Thomas Council, 18470 W. Ten Mile Rd., Southfield, MI 48075
- Chaldean Sisters, Daughters of Mary Immaculate, 19138 Danbury, Detroit, Michigan 48203
  (313) 368-7999
- Mar Addai Chaldean Parish, 24010 Coolidge Hwy., Oak Park, MI 48237; (248) 547-4648
- Our Lady of Chaldeans Cathedral (Mother of God Church), 25063 Berg Rd., Southfield, MI 48034; (248) 356-0565

- Sacred Heart Chaldean Parish, 310 W. Seven Mile Rd., Detroit, MI 48203; (313) 368-6214
- St. George Chaldean Church, Shelby Township, MI
- St. Joseph Chaldean Parish, 2442 Big Beaver Rd., Troy, MI 48083; (248) 528-3676
- St. Thomas Chaldean Parish, 6900 Maple Rd., West Bloomfield, MI 48322; (248) 788-2460

Secular Chaldean Community Organizations

- Arab-American and Chaldean Council, 28551 Southfield Rd., Suite 204, Lathrup Village, MI 48076; (248) 559-1990
- Associated Food Dealers of Michigan, 18470 W. Ten Mile Rd., Southfield, MI 48075; (800) 66-66-AFD or (248) 557-9600
- Chaldean-American Ladies of Charity, 25626 Telegraph Rd., Southfield, MI 48034; (248) 352-9020
- Chaldean-Iraqi Association of Michigan ("CIAAM") (Social and Cultural Organization of Chaldeans), Southfield Manor, 25626 Telegraph Rd., Southfield, MI 48034-7403; (248) 352-9020
- Chaldean Federation of America (Umbrella association of Chaldean organizations in the United States), 18740 W. Ten Mile Rd., Southfield, MI 48075; (248) 557-3262; *http://www.chaldeandiocese.org/chaldeanfederation.com/*
- *The Chaldean News*, 30095 Northwestern Highway, Suite 102, Farmington Hills, MI 48334; (248) 932-3100; *www.chaldeannews.com*
- Detroit Middle East Newspaper, 21419 John R, Hazel Park, MI 48030; (248) 543-5583
- Mid-East Media, 21419 John R, Hazel Park, MI 48030; (248) 543-5583; *Salah@mideastradio.net*
- Shenandoah Country Club (associated with the Chaldean-Iraqi Association of Michigan and future location of planned Chaldean Cultural Center), 5600 Walnut Lake Rd., West Bloomfield, MI 48323; (248) 683-6363

Other Related Web Sites

- On the Aramaic/Asssyrian/Chaldean Language: *http://members
  .aol.com/assyrianme/aramaic/aramaic.html*
- On Assyrian History, History of Nineveh: *http://www.nineveh.com/*
- Individual Site on Chaldeans with Chat Room: *http://members
  .aol.com/chaldeans7/*

Notes

1. R. Karoukian, "47e Recountre Assyriologique Internationale," *Nineveh* 24, no. 3 (2001): 1–2.
2. See map; see also M. Bazzi, *Chaldeans Past and Present*, 2d ed. (San Diego, Calif.: St. Peter Chaldean Catholic Church, 1991).
3. "Mesopotamia, History of," *Encyclopædia Britannica*, CD-ROM Edition, 2001.
4. M. C. Sengstock, *Chaldean-Americans: Changing Conceptions of Ethnic Identity*, 2d ed. (New York: Center for Migration Studies, 1999). For further discussion of the history of the Chaldeans and Iraq, see, for example, G. S. Goodspeed, *A History of the Babylonians and the Assyrians* (New York: Scribners, 1902); Roux, *Ancient Iraq;* A. D. Jaddou and A. O. Jamil, *The Heirs of Mesopotamia: Chaldeans and Assyrians* (Southfield, Mich.: Chaldean Academy Publications, 1995); and S. Y. H. Jammo, "Chaldeans of Metropolitan Detroit," in *Chaldean Directory, 1982–83*, 15th ed. (Southfield and East Detroit, Mich.: Chaldean Catholic Church of America and Stephen's NU-AD, Inc., 1982–83), 8–12.
5. Sengstock, *Chaldean-Americans*, 2d ed.
6. Ibid.
7. Ibid.
8. B. C. Aswad, "Introduction and Overview," in *Arabic-Speaking Communities*

in American Cities, ed. B. C. Aswad (New York: Center for Migration Studies and Association of Arab-American University Graduates, 1974); M. C. Sengstock, "Telkaif, Baghdad, Detroit—Chaldeans Blend Three Cultures," *Michigan History* 54 (1970): 293–310.; M. C. Sengstock, *Chaldean-Americans: Changing Conceptions of Ethnic Identity,* 2d ed. (New York: Center for Migration Studies, 1999); W. P. Adeney, *The Greek and Eastern Churches* (Clifton, N.J.: Reference Book Publishers, 1965).

9. Sengstock, *Chaldean-Americans,* 2d ed. .

10. Ibid.

11. Douglas S. Massey, "The New Immigration and Ethnicity in the United States," *Population and Development Review* 21, no. 3 (September 1995): 631–52.

12. Research Department, *A Study of the Middle East Community in the Detroit Metropolitan Area* (Detroit: United Community Services of Metropolitan Detroit, 1986), 38.

13. A. Naff, "Arabs in America: A Historical Overview," in *Arabs in the New World,* ed. S. Y. Abraham and N. Abraham, 89 (Detroit: Wayne State University Center for Urban Studies, 1983).

14. Research Department, *Middle East Community,* 19. See also J. Zogby, *Arab-America Today: A Demographic Profile of Arab Americans* (Washington, D.C.: Arab-American Institute, 1990), for a discussion of the Arab-speaking population in the United States.

15. S. Jammo, "Contemporary Chaldeans' Origin and Ethnicity with special regard to their presence in the U.S.A." (presentation to the Chaldean Federation of America—Census 2000 Committee, Southfield, Mich., May 12, 1998); Sengstock, *Chaldean-Americans,* 2d ed.

16. Jammo, "Origin and Ethnicity"

17. Church officials know from experience that they typically receive a certain number of requests for weddings, funerals, baptisms, and so on, from the community they serve. The priest is assuming that an increase in the number of such requests indicates a similar increase in the size of the population.

18. R. A. Lochore, *From Europe to New Zealand* (Wellington: Institute of Political Affairs,1951), 23–25; J. S. MacDonald and L. MacDonald, "Urbanization, Ethnic Groups, and Social Segregation," *Social Research* 29 (1962): 433–48; J. S. MacDonald and L. MacDonald, "Chain Migration, Ethnic Neighborhood Formation, and Social Networks," *Millbank Memorial Fund*

Quarterly 42 (1964): 82–97; and B. Thompson, "Newcomers to the City: Factors Influencing Initial Settlement and Ethnic Community Growth Patterns," in *Immigrants and Migrants: The Detroit Ethnic Experience,* ed. D. Hartman (Detroit: Wayne State University Week-End College, 1974).

19. S. N. Eisenstadt, "The Process of Absorption of New Immigrants in Israel," *Human Relations* 5 (1952): 225.

20. M. C. Sengstock, *Chaldean-Americans: Changing Conceptions of Ethnic Identity,* 1st ed. (New York: Center for Migration Studies, 1982).

21. S. K. Farsoun, "Family Structure and Society in Modern Lebanon," in *Peoples and Cultures of the Middle East,* vol. 2, ed. L. E. Sweet (Garden City, N.Y.: Natural History Press, 1970), 257.

22. Robert Ankony, "American Dreamers," *Crain's Detroit Business,* March 29, 1999.

23. In the 1990–91 study of Chaldean elders, over half of the respondents reported having frequent contact with relatives outside the United States. Some listed as many as thirty such relatives, and many reported making financial contributions to them. Respondents often list a relative as their "closest friend" (Sengstock, *Chaldean-Americans,* 2d ed.).

24. Amy Lane, "American Dreamers," *Crain's Detroit Business,* March 29, 1999.

25. H. J. Gans, *The Urban Villagers* (New York: The Free Press of Glencoe, 1962).

26. Bazzi, *Chaldeans Past.*

27. For a discussion of some other Arabic-speaking communities in the United States, see S. Y. Abraham, "A Survey of the Arab-American Community in Metropolitan Detroit," in *The Arab World and Arab-Americans: Understanding a Neglected Minority* (Detroit: University Center for Urban Studies, 1981); S. Y. Abraham, "Detroit's Arab-American Community: A Survey of Diversity and Commonality," in *Arabs in the New World,* ed. S. Y. Abraham and N. Abraham (Detroit: Wayne State University Center for Urban Studies, 1983); B. Abu-Laban, "The Arab-Canadian Community," in *The Arab-Americans,* ed. E. C. Hagopian and A. Paden (Wilmette, Ill.: Medina University Press International, 1969); and B. C. Aswad, and B. Bilge, eds., *Family and Gender Among American Muslims* (Philadelphia, Penn., Temple University Press, 1997).

28. Sarhad Jammo, "Contemporary Chaldeans and Assyrians: Our Primordial Nation, One Original Church," *Chaldean Directory 2000–2001,* 19th ed. (Eastpointe, Mich.: Cal Press, 2000), 26–41.

29. Ibid.

30. Ibid.

31. Ibid.

32. For historical background on early controversies in the Christian Church, see W. P. Adeney, *The Greek and Eastern Churches* (Clifton, N.J.: Reference Book Publishers, 1965); D. Attwater, *Eastern Catholic Worship* (New York: Devin-Adair, 1945); D. Attwater, *The Christian Churches of the East*, rev. ed., 2 vols. (Milwaukee, Wisc.: Bruce Publishing Co., 1947); D. Attwater, *Churches in Communion with Rome*, vol. 1 of *Christian Churches of the East* (New York: Bruce, 1961–62); R. Rabban, "Chaldean Rite," *New Catholic Encyclopedia* (New York: McGraw-Hill, 1967), 3:427–30; S. Colbi, 1969; *Christianity in the Holy Land, Past and Present* (Tel Aviv: Am Hassefer, 1969); R. M. Haddad, *Syrian Christians in Muslim Society* (Princeton, N.J.: Princeton University Press, 1970); J. Perkins, "Journal Reports," *Missionary Herald*, 5 January–5 December 1837, 7–307; Jammo, "Origin and Ethnicity"; and Jammo, "Chaldeans and Assyrians."

33. It should be noted, however, that there probably is as much similarity between modern Aramaic and the language of Jesus as there is between American English and the English of *Beowulf.*

34. Jaddou, and Jamil, *Heirs of Mesopotamia;* Sarhad Jammo, *Chaldean Language: Elementary Course* (Troy, Mich.: Saint Joseph Chaldean Catholic Parish, 1996); Jacob Yasso and Amer Hanna Fatuhi, *Chaldean English Arabic Picture Dictionary* (Detroit: The Chaldean Educational Center, 2002); Mary Yousif, *Chaldean Reading Book, Beginners* (Detroit: Chaldean Cultural Center of America, 2003).

35. Joseph Hraba, *American Ethnicity* (Itasca, Ill.: Peacock, 1994).

36. For a discussion of comparable economic patterns in other ethnic communities, see Edna Bonacich, "A Theory of Middleman Minorities," *American Sociological Review* 38 (October 1973): 547–59; Edna Bonacich, "Class Approaches to Ethnicity and Race," *Insurgent Sociologist* 19 (Fall 1980): 11; Edna Bonacich and John Modell, *The Economic Basis of Ethnic Solidarity* (Berkeley: University of California Press, 1980); Joe R. Feagin and Clairece Booher Feagin, *Racial and Ethnic Relations*, 5th ed. (Englewood Cliffs, N.J.: Prentice-Hall, 1996); Hraba, *American Ethnicity*, 1994; I. Light and E. Bonacich, *Immigrant Entrepreneurs: Koreans in Los Angeles, 1965–1982* (Berkeley: University of California Press, 1988); and Pyong Gap

Min, *Caught in the Middle* (Berkeley, Calif.: University of California Press, 1996).

37. For a more extensive analysis of the Chaldean grocery business, see M. C. Sengstock, "Iraqi-Christians in Detroit: An Analysis of an Ethnic Occupation," in *Arabic-Speaking Communities in American Cities,* ed. B. C. Aswad (New York: Center for Migration Studies and Association of Arab-American University Graduates, 1974); M. C. Sengstock, *Chaldean-Americans,* 2d ed. .

38. Lane, "American Dreamers"; Ankony, "American Dreamers."

39. MacDonald and MacDonald, "Urbanization"; 1964; Massey, "New Immigration"; and E. S. Lee, "Theory of Migration," *Demography* 3, no. 1 (1966): 47–57.

40. Arthur Bridgeforth Jr., "More Competition in Store as Kroger Plans Detroit Entry," *Crain's Detroit Business,* 16 August 1999; Brent Snavely, "Food Fight: Kroger, Farmer Jack Square Off," *Crain's Detroit Business,* 21 May 2001.

41. Sengstock, *Chaldean-Americans,* 2d ed.

42. Donald E. Gelfand, *Aging and Ethnicity* (New York: Springer, 1994).

43. E. C. Ravenstein, "The Laws of Migration," *Journal of the Royal Statistical Society* 48, no. 2 (1885): 167–227; E. C. Ravenstein, "The Laws of Migration," *Journal of the Royal Statistical Society* 52 (June 1889): 241–301; and Lee, "Theory of Migration."

44. M. Hussain, "Children Suffering," *Detroit Sunday Journal,* March 22, 1998, 9; Sengstock, *Chaldean-Americans,* 2d ed.

45. "Detroit-Baghdad Connection," *Chaldean News* 1, no. 8 (September 2004): 14.

46. Massey, "New Immigration"; Thomas J. Espenshade, "Unauthorized Immigration to the United States," *Annual Review of Sociology* 21 (1995): 195–216.

47. Massey, "New Immigration"; R. Tomlinson, *Demographic Problems* (Belmont, Calif.: Dickenson, 1997); R. C. Alexander, "A Defense of the McCarran-Walter Act," *Law and Contemporary Problems* 21 (Spring 1956): 382–400.

48. Crystal C. Jabiro, "Strengthening Our Chaldean Families," *Chaldean News* 1, no. 3 (April 2004): 21, 30.

49. Sengstock, *Chaldean-Americans,* 2d ed.

50. J. C. Cavanaugh, *Adult Development and Aging* (Belmont, Calif: Wadsworth, 1990); Gelfand, *Aging and Ethnicity.*

51. For a discussion of the role of family care-giving, see R. E. Young and E. Kahana, "Specifying Caregiver Outcomes: Gender and Relationship Aspects of Caregiving Strain," *Gerontologist* 29 (1989): 660–66; E. P. Stoller, "Males as Helpers: The Role of Sons, Relatives and Friends," *Gerontologist* 30 (1990): 228–35; E. M. Brody, *Women in the Middle: Their Parent-Care Years* (New York: Springer, 1990); S. H. Mathews and T. T. Rosner, "Shared Filial Responsibility: The Family as the Primary Caregiver," *Journal of Marriage and the Family* 50 (1998): 185–95; T. H. Brubaker and E. Brubaker, "Family Care of the Elderly in the United States: An Issue of Gender Differences?" in *Family Care of the Elderly*, ed. J. I. Kosberg (Newbury Park, Calif.: Sage, 1992): 210–31.

52. For a discussion of the Arab nationalist movement, see, for example, L. S. El-Hamamsy, "The Assertion of Egyptian Identity," in *Arab Society in Transition*, ed. S. E. Ibrahim and N. S. Hopkins (Cairo: American University in Cairo, 1977); A. H. Hourani, *Syria and Lebanon* (London: Oxford University Press, 1946); and Fouad Ajamy, "The End of Arab Nationalism," *New Republic* 105 (12 August 1991): 23–27.

53. For more discussion of the impact of the Gulf War on Arabic-speaking communities in the United States, see Peter Applebome, "Arab-Americans Fear a Land War's Backlash," *New York Times*, 20 February 1991, A1, A8; Thomas J. Espenshade and Katherine Hempstead, "Contemporary American Attitudes Toward U.S. Immigration," *International Migration Review* 30, no. 2 (Summer 1996): 535–70; Sara Diamond, "Right-Wing Politics and the Anti-Immigration Cause," *Social Justice* 23, no. 3 (Fall 1996): 154–68; C. Cook and J. Schaefer, "Arson Called Evidence of Anti-Arab Feelings," *Detroit Free Press*, January 31, 1991, B-1; P. Edmonds, "Hate Crimes Grow: Arab Americans Say the Rate Has Jumped Since War Began," *Detroit Free Press*, 7 February 1991, 3, 4A; Michael Betzold, "Iraqis in Detroit," *Detroit Sunday Journal*, March 1, 1998, 1, 6; Michael Betzold, "The Media, the War and the Bottom Line." *Detroit Sunday Journal*, March 1, 1998, 7; and J. Zaslow, "How a Rumor Spread by Email Laid Low an Arab's Restaurant," *Wall Street Journal*, 13 March 2002, A1, 9.

54. Marsha Stoppa, "Local Dairy among Three Charged by State," *Crain's Detroit Business*, November 7, 1994; Marsha Stoppa, "Melody Execs Won't Sue Feds—An 'Unusual' Move," *Crain's Detroit Business*, November 10, 1997.

55. Gregg Krupa, "Area Chaldeans Fear for Families in Iraq," *Detroit News*, August 13, 2004, 1, 10A.

56. Jeffrey J. Atto, "An Open Letter to *The Chaldean News*," *Chaldean News* 1, no. 3 (April 2004): 5.

57. Omar Binno and Vanessa Denha, "Rebuilding a Homeland," *Chaldean News* 1, no. 5 (June 2004): 18–19, 25; "A Democratic Iraq?" *Chaldean News* 1, no. 5 (June 2004): 20.; Dan Senor, "Charting Iraq's Progress," *Chaldean News* 1, no. 5 (June 2004): 17, 40; "New Constitution Points Iraq in the Right Direction," *Chaldean News* 1, no. 3 (April 2004): 6.

58. Vanessa Denha, "What Now?" *Chaldean News* 1, no. 8 (September 2004): 20–21; "Iraqi Leaders Condemn Church Bombings," *Chaldean News* 1, no. 8 (September 2004): 12.

59. "Future of the Iraqi Government?" *Chaldean News* 1, no. 5 (June 2004): 16.

60. Vanessa Denha, "What Now?" *Chaldean News* 1, no. 8 (September 2004): 20–21.

61. Tom Lasseter and Dogan Hannah, "Bombs Tear Open Five Iraqi Churches," *Detroit Free Press*, August 2, 2004, 1; "Assyrian Compound Mortared," *Chaldean News* 1, no. 8 (September 2004): 12; "Christians Fear Further Persecution," *Chaldean News* 1, no. 8 (September 2004): 13; "Church Bombing Victims," *Chaldean News* 1, no. 8 (September 2004): 13; Vanessa Denha, "What Now?" *Chaldean News* 1, no. 8 (September 2004): 20–21; "Detroit-Baghdad Connection," *Chaldean News* 1, no. 8 (September 2004): 14; "Iraqi Leaders Condemn Church Bombings," *Chaldean News* 1, no. 8 (September 2004): 12; "A Week After Bombings, Chaldeans Worship Cautiously," *Chaldean News* 1, no. 8 (September 2004): 13, 14.

62. "The New Iraqi Flag" *Chaldean News* 1, no. 5 (June 2004): 7.

63. Kristin Palm, "Arab Market a Target Businesses Haven't Hit," *Crain's Detroit Business*, August 8, 1999.

64. *Chaldean Directory, 2000–2001*, 19th ed. (Eastpointe, Mich.: Cal Press, 2000), 298; Diane Dickow D'Agostini, "It's Your Duty," *Chaldean News* 1, no. 3 (April 2004): 26.

65. Bridgeforth, "More Competition."

66. Ibid.; Snavely, "Food Fight."

67. Bridgeforth, "More Competition"; Joseph Serwach, "Farmer Jack Plans to Build 8 Stores, Most Local," *Crain's Detroit Business*, March 17, 1997; Snavely, "Food Fight."

68. Ankony, "American Dreamers."

69. Arthur Bridgeforth Jr., "Cards Deal Marketing Edge to Supermarkets," *Crain's Detroit Business*, September 27, 1999.

70. Ankony, "American Dreamers."

71. Stopa, "Melody Execs."

72. Paul Gargaro and David Barkholz, "Providence Chooses Jonna to Develop 65-Acre Novi Site," *Crain's Detroit Business*, November 3, 1997.

73. See Gary David, "Behind the Counter: Iraqi-Chaldean Store Ownership in Metropolitan Detroit," in *Arab Detroit: From Margin to Mainstream*, ed. N. Abraham and A. Shyrock (Detroit: Wayne State University Press, 1999), for a discussion of these problems.

74. For additional information about the contrasting views of Chaldeans and suburban school districts see A. M. Doctoroff, "The Chaldeans: A New Ethnic Group in Detroit's Suburban High Schools" (Ph.D. diss., University of Michigan, 1978)."Hate Crimes Grow: Arab Americans Say the Rate Has Jumped Since War Began," *Detroit Free Press*, 7 February 1991, 3, 4A; Michael Betzold, "Iraqis in Detroit," *Detroit Sunday Journal*, March 1, 1998, 1, 6; Michael Betzold, "The Media, the War and the Bottom Line," *Detroit Sunday Journal*, March 1, 1998, 7; and J. Zaslow, "How a Rumor Spread by Email Laid Low an Arab's Restaurant," *Wall Street Journal*, 13 March 2002, A1, 9.

For Further Reference

Abraham, S. Y. "Detroit's Arab-American Community: A Survey of Diversity and Commonality." In *Arabs in the New World,* ed. S.Y. Abraham and N. Abraham. Detroit: Wayne State University Center for Urban Studies, 1983.

———."A Survey of the Arab-American Community in Metropolitan Detroit." In *The Arab World and Arab-Americans: Understanding a Neglected Minority,* ed. S. Y. Abraham and N. Abraham. Detroit: University Center for Urban Studies, 1981.

Abu-Laban, B. "The Arab-Canadian Community." In *The Arab Americans,* ed. E. C. Hagopian and A. Paden. Wilmette, Ill.: Medina University Press International, 1969.

Abu-Laban, B., and F. T. Zeadey. *Arabs in America: Myths and Realities.* Wilmette, Ill.: Medina, 1975.

Adeney, W. P. *The Greek and Eastern Churches.* Clifton, N.J.: Reference Book Publishers, 1965.

Ajami, Fouad. "The End of Arab Nationalism." *New Republic* 105 (12 August 1991): 23–27.

Alexander, R. C. 1956. "A Defense of the McCarran-Walter Act." *Law and Contemporary Problems* 21 (Spring): 382–400.

Ankony, Robert. "American Dreamers." *Crain's Detroit Business,* March 29, 1999.

Applebome, Peter. "Arab-Americans Fear a Land War's Backlash." *New York Times* (February 20, 1991): A1, A8.

"Assyrian Compound Mortared." *Chaldean News* 1, no. 8 (September 2004): 12.

Aswad, B. C. "Introduction and Overview." In *Arabic-Speaking Communities in American Cities*, ed. B. C. Aswad. New York: Center for Migration Studies and Association of Arab-American University Graduates, 1974.

Aswad, B. C., and B. Bilge, eds. *Family and Gender Among American Muslims.* Philadelphia, Penn.: Temple University Press, 1997.

Atto, Jeffrey J. "An Open Letter to *The Chaldean News.*" *Chaldean News* 1, no. 3 (April 2004): 5.

Attwater, D. *The Christian Churches of the East.* Rev. ed. 2 vols. Milwaukee, Wisc.: Bruce Publishing Co., 1947.

———. *Churches in Communion with Rome.* Vol. 1 of Christian Churches of the East. New York: Bruce, 1961–62.

———. *Eastern Catholic Worship.* New York: Devin-Adair, 1945.

Bazzi, M. *Chaldeans Past and Present.* 2d ed. San Diego, Calif.: St. Peter Chaldean Catholic Church, 1991.

———. "Chaldeans Present and Past." In *Chaldean Directory,* 17th ed. Southfield and East Detroit, Mich.: Chaldean Diocese in the United States of America and Stephen's NU-AD, 1991.

Betzold, Michael. "Iraqis in Detroit." *Detroit Sunday Journal,* 3, no. 16 (March 1, 1998): 1, 6.

———. "The Media, the War and the Bottom Line." *Detroit Sunday Journal* 3, no. 16 (March 1, 1998): 7.

Binno, Omar, and Vanessa Denha. "Rebuilding a Homeland." *Chaldean News* 1, no. 5 (June 2004): 18–19, 25.

Bonacich, Edna. "Class Approaches to Ethnicity and Race." *Insurgent Sociologist* 10 (Fall 1980): 11.

———. "A Theory of Middleman Minorities." *American Sociological Review* 38 (October 1973): 547–59.

Bonacich, Edna, and John Modell. *The Economic Basis of Ethnic Solidarity.* Berkeley, Calif.: University of California Press, 1980.

Bridgeforth, Arthur, Jr. "Cards Deal Marketing Edge to Supermarkets." *Crain's Detroit Business,* September 27, 1999.

———. "More Competition in Store as Kroger Plans Detroit Entry." *Crain's Detroit Business,* August 16, 1999.

Brody, E. M. *Women in the Middle: Their Parent-Care Years.* New York: Springer, 1990.

Brubaker, T. H., and Brubaker, E. "Family Care of the Elderly in the United States: An Issue of Gender Differences?" In *Family Care of the Elderly.* Ed. J. I. Kosberg. Newbury Park, Calif.: Sage, 1992.

Cavanaugh, J. C. *Adult Development and Aging.* Belmont, Calif.: Wadsworth, 1990.

Calendar of the Chaldean People of Ancient Babylonia. Detroit, Mich.: Chaldean Educational Center in Metropolitan Detroit, 2002.

Chaldean Directory, 1999. 17th ed. Eastpointe, Mich.: Cal Press, 1999.

Chaldean Directory, 2000–2001. 19th ed. Eastpointe, Mich.: Cal Press, 2000.

"Christians Fear Further Persecution." *Chaldean News* 1, no. 8 (September 2004): 13.

"Church Bombing Victims." *Chaldean News* 1, no. 8 (September 2004): 13.

Colbi, S. *Christianity in the Holy Land, Past and Present.* Tel Aviv: Am Hassefer, 1969.

Cook, C., and Schaefer, J.. "Arson Called Evidence of Anti-Arab Feelings." *Detroit Free Press,* January 31, 1991, B-1.

D'Agostini, Diane Dickow. "It's Your Duty." *Chaldean News* 1, no. 3 (April 2004).

David, Gary. "Behind the Counter: Iraqi-Chaldean Store Ownership in Metropolitan Detroit." In *Arab Detroit: From Margin to Mainstream,* ed. N. Abraham and A. Shyrock. Detroit, Mich.: Wayne State University Press, 1999.

"A Democratic Iraq?" *Chaldean News* 1, no. 5 (June 2004): 20.

Denha, Vanessa. "Celebrating a Rebirth." *Chaldean News* 1, no. 4 (April 2004): 18–19, 25.

———. "What Now?" *Chaldean News* 1, no. 8 (September 2004): 20–21.

"Detroit-Baghdad Connection." *Chaldean News* 1, no. 8 (September 2004): 14.

Diamond, Sara. "Right-Wing Politics and the Anti-Immigration Cause." *Social Justice* 23, no. 3 (Fall 1996): 154–68.

Doctoroff, A. M. "The Chaldeans: A New Ethnic Group in Detroit's Suburban High Schools." Ph.D. dissertation. University of Michigan, 1978.

Edmonds, P. "Hate Crimes Grow: Arab Americans Say the Rate Has Jumped Since War Began." *Detroit Free Press* (7 February 1991): 3, 4A.

Eisenstadt, S. N. "The Process of Absorption of New Immigrants in Israel." *Human Relations* 5 (1952): 223–46.

El-Hamamsy, L. S. "The Assertion of Egyptian Identity." In *Arab Society in Transition*, ed. S. E. Ibrahim and N. S. Hopkins. Cairo: American University in Cairo, 1977.

Espenshade, Thomas J. "Unauthorized Immigration to the United States." *Annual Review of Sociology* 21 (1995): 195–216.

Espenshade, Thomas J., and Katherine Hempstead. "Contemporary American Attitudes toward U.S. Immigration." *International Migration Review* 30, no. 2 (Summer 1996): 535–70.

Farsoun, S. K. "Family Structure and Society in Modern Lebanon." In *Peoples and Cultures of the Middle East*, vol. 2, ed. L. E. Sweet. Garden City, N.Y.: Natural History Press, 1970.

Feagin, Joe R., and Clairece Booher Feagin. *Racial and Ethnic Relations*. 5th ed. Englewood Cliffs, N.J.: Prentice-Hall, 1996.

"Future of the Iraqi Governmnent?" *Chaldean News* 1, no. 5 (June 2004): 16.

Gans, H. J. *The Urban Villagers*. New York: The Free Press of Glencoe, 1962.

Gargaro, Paul, and David Barkholz. "Providence Chooses Jonna to Develop 65-Acre Novi Site." *Crain's Detroit Business*, November 3, 1997.

Gelfand, Donald E. *Aging and Ethnicity*. New York: Springer, 1994.

Goodspeed, G. S. *A History of the Babylonians and the Assyrians*. New York: Scribners, 1902.

Gutierrez, Luis. "The New Assault on Immigrants." *Social Policy* 25, no. 4 (Summer 1995): 56–63.

Haddad, R. M. *Syrian Christians in Muslim Society*. Princeton, N J.: Princeton University Press, 1970.

Hourani, A. H. *Syria and Lebanon*. London: Oxford University Press, 1946.

Hraba, Joseph. *American Ethnicity*. Itasca, Ill.: Peacock, 1994.

Hussain, M. "Children Suffering." *Detroit Sunday Journal*, March 22, 1998.

"Iraqi Leaders Condemn Church Bombings." *Chaldean News* 1, no. 8 (September 2004): 12

Jabiro, Crystal C. "Strengthening Our Chaldean Families." *Chaldean News* 1, no. 3 (April 2004): 21, 30.

Jaddou, A. D., and A. O. Jamil. *The Heirs of Mesopotamia: Chaldeans and Assyrians*. Southfield, Mich.: Chaldean Academy Publications, 1995.

Jammo, Sarhad. *Chaldean Language: Elementary Course*. Troy, Mich.: Saint Joseph Chaldean Catholic Parish, 1996.

———. "Chaldeans of Metropolitan Detroit." In *Chaldean Directory*, 1982–83.

15th ed. Southfield and East Detroit, Mich.: Chaldean Catholic Church of America and Stephen's NU-AD, 1982–83.

———. "Contemporary Chaldeans and Assyrians: Our Primordial Nation, One Original Church." In *Chaldean Directory 2000–2001*. 19th ed. Eastpointe, Mich.: Cal Press, 2000.

———. "Contemporary Chaldeans' Origin and Ethnicity with Special regard to Their Presence in the U.S.A." Southfield, Mich.: Presentation to the Chaldean Federation of America—Census 2000 Committee, May 12, 1998.

Karoukian, R. "47e Recountre Assyriologique Internationale." *Nineveh* 24, no. 3 (2001): 1–2

Krupa, Gregg. "Area Chaldeans Fear for Families in Iraq." *Detroit News* (August 13, 2004): 1, 10A.

Lane, Amy. "American Dreamers." *Crain's Detroit Business*, March 29, 1999.

Lasseter, Tom, and Dogan Hannah. "Bombs Tear Open Five Iraqi Churches." *Detroit Free Press* (August 2, 2004): 1.

Lee, E. S. "Theory of Migration," *Demography*, 3, no. 1 (1966): 47–57.

Light, I., and E. Bonacich. *Immigrant Entrepreneurs: Koreans in Los Angeles, 1965–1982*. Berkeley: University of California Press, 1988.

Lochore, R. A. *From Europe to New Zealand*. Wellington, N.Z.: Institute of Political Affairs, 1951.

MacDonald, J. S., and L. MacDonald. "Chain Migration, Ethnic Neighborhood Formation, and Social Networks." *Milbank Memorial Fund Quarterly* 42 (1964): 82–97.

———. "Urbanization, Ethnic Groups, and Social Segregation." *Social Research* 29 (1962): 433–48.

Mathews, S. H., and Rosner, T. T. "Shared Filial Responsibility: The Family as the Primary Caregiver." *Journal of Marriage and the Family* 50 (1998): 185–95.

Massey, Douglas S. "The New Immigration and Ethnicity in the United States." *Population and Development Review* 21, no. 3 (September 1995): 631–52.

"Mesopotamia, History of." *Encyclopaedia Britannica*. CD-ROM ed., 2001.

"Mesopotamian Religion." *Encyclopaedia Britannica*. CD-ROM ed., 2001.

Min, Pyong Gap. *Caught in the Middle*. Berkeley, Calif.: University of California Press, 1996.

Naff, A. "Arabs in America: A Historical Overview." In *Arabs in the New World*, ed. S. Y. Abraham and N. Abraham. Detroit: Wayne State University Center for Urban Studies, 1983.

Najor, Julia. *Babylonian Cuisine: Chaldean Cookbook from the Middle East.* 2d ed. Detroit, Mich.: National Books International, 1981.

"New Constitution Points Iraq in the Right Direction." *Chaldean News* 1, no. 3 (April 2004): 6.

"The New Iraqi Flag." *Chaldean News* 1, no. 5 (June 2004).

Olmstead, A. T. *History of Assyria.* New York: Charles Scribner and Sons, 1923.

Oppenheim, A. L. *Ancient Mesopotamia.* Rev. ed. Chicago: University of Chicago Press, 1977.

Palm, Kristen. "Arab Market a Target Businesses Haven't Hit." *Crain's Detroit Business,* August 8, 1999.

Parrillo, Vincent N. "Diversity in America: A Sociohistorical Analysis." *Sociological Focus* 9, no. 4 (1994): 523–45.

Perkins, J. "Journal Reports," *Missionary Herald* 5 January–5 December 1837): 7–307.

Rabban R. "Chaldean Rite." *New Catholic Encyclopedia* New York: McGraw-Hill, 1987, 3:427–30.

Ravenstein, E. C. "The Laws of Migration." *Journal of the Royal Statistical Society* 48 (June 1885): 167–227.

———. "The Laws of Migration." *Journal of the Royal Statistical Society* 52 (June 1889): 241–301.

Roux, G. *Ancient Iraq.* Rev. ed. Middlesex, England: Penguin, 1976.

Sengstock, M. C. *Chaldean-Americans: Changing Conceptions of Ethnic Identity.* 1st ed. New York: Center for Migration Studies, 1982.

———. *Chaldean-Americans: Changing Conceptions of Ethnic Identity.* 2d ed. New York: Center for Migration Studies, 1999.

———. "Iraqi-Christians in Detroit: An Analysis of an Ethnic Occupation." In *Arabic-Speaking Communities in American Cities,* ed. B. C. Aswad. New York: Center for Migration Studies and Association of Arab-American University Graduates, 1974.

———. "Telkaif, Baghdad, Detroit—Chaldeans Blend Three Cultures." *Michigan History* 54 (1970): 293–310.

Senor, Dan. "Charting Iraq's Progress." *Chaldean News* 1, no. 5 (June 2004): 17, 40.

Serwach, Joseph. "Farmer Jack Plans to Build Eight Stores, Most Local." *Crain's Detroit Business,* March 17, 1997.

Simon, R. J. "Old Minorities, New Immigrants: Aspirations, Hopes, and Fears."

Annals of the American Academy of Political and Social Science 530 (November 1993): 61–73.

Snavely, Brent. "Food Fight: Kroger, Farmer Jack Square Off." *Crain's Detroit Business,* May 21, 2001.

Stoller, E. P. "Males as Helpers: The Role of Sons, Relatives and Friends." *Gerontologist* 30 (1990): 228–35

Stopa, Marsha. "Local Dairy among Three Charged by State." *Crain's Detroit Business,* November 7, 1994.

———. "Melody Execs Won't Sue Feds—An 'Unusual' Move." *Crain's Detroit Business,* November 10, 1997.

A Study of the Middle East Community in the Detroit Metropolitan Area. Detroit: United Community Services of Metropolitan Detroit, 1986.

Thompson, B. "Newcomers to the City: Factors Influencing Initial Settlement and Ethnic Community Growth Patterns." In *Immigrants and Migrants: The Detroit Ethnic Experience,* ed. D. Hartman. Detroit: Wayne State University Week-End College, 1974.

Tomlinson, R. *Demographic Problems.* Belmont, Calif.: Dickenson, 1997.

"A Week After Bombings, Chaldeans Worship Cautiously." *Chaldean News* 1, no. 8 (September 2004): 13, 14.

Yasso, Jacob, and Fatuhi, Amer Hanna. *Chaldean English Arabic Picture Dictionary.* Detroit: The Chaldean Educational Center, 2002.

Young, R. E., and E. Kahana. "Specifying Caregiver Outcomes: Gender and Relationship Aspects of Caregiving Strain." *Gerontologist* 29 (1989): 660–66

Yousif, Mary. Chaldean Reading Book, Beginners. Detroit: Chaldean Cultural Center of America, 2003.

Zaslow, J. "How a Rumor Spread by Email Laid Low an Arab's Restaurant." *Wall Street Journal* 239, no. 50 (March 13, 2002): A1, 9.

Zogby, J. *Arab-America Today: A Demographic Profile of Arab Americans.* Washington, D.C.: Arab-American Institute, 1990.

Index